# Street Kid Fights On

ALSO BY JUDY WESTWATER

Street Kid

# Street Kid Fights On

**She thought the nightmare was over**

## JUDY WESTWATER

THE BESTSELLING AUTHOR OF *STREET KID*

This is a work of non-fiction. In order to protect privacy, some names and details have been changed.

HarperElement
An Imprint of HarperCollins*Publishers*
77–85 Fulham Palace Road,
Hammersmith, London W6 8JB

The website address is:
www.thorsonselement.com

and *HarperElement* are trademarks of
HarperCollins*Publishers* Ltd

First published by HarperElement 2008

1 3 5 7 9 10 8 6 4 2

A catalogue record of this book
is available from the British Library

ISBN-13 978-0-00-726662-3 (hardback)
ISBN-10 0-00-726662-6 (hardback)
ISBN-13 978-0-00-726663-0 (paperback)
ISBN-10 0-00-726663-4 (paperback)

Printed and bound in Great Britain by
Clays Ltd, St Ives plc

**Mixed Sources**
Product group from well-managed
forests and other controlled sources
www.fsc.org   Cert no. SW-COC-1806
© 1996 Forest Stewardship Council
FSC

FOR ALL SURVIVORS

Hold fast that strength of courage

# Prologue

I never had anyone looking after me – I always just looked after myself from when I was very young.

My father, a phoney spiritualist preacher, used me as a punch bag from the day he abducted me as a two-year-old from his estranged wife's home in a spiteful gesture of revenge. His partner Freda treated me like her slave, starving and beating me daily and locking me out in the back yard in all weathers. Things weren't any better when they took me to live in South Africa then abandoned me, so that I ended up sleeping rough on the streets of Johannesburg at the age of twelve. When I was seventeen, I came back to the UK to look for my Mum but found she didn't want to have anything to do with me; she and my sisters had their own lives to lead by then.

I was pretty streetwise and knew how to keep myself alive. I wouldn't starve or die of cold so long as I could forage in dustbins for food and find an old shack to sleep in. But I didn't have a clue about how normal human relationships worked. I didn't have any social skills or instincts about character. If someone was nice to me, I thought that meant they were a good person and I gave them my trust.

If they treated me badly, I thought it was my fault, that I must have done something wrong. As for love, I didn't know what that meant.

A whole new learning curve was about to begin.

# Chapter One

The advert in the *Manchester Evening News* read: 'Trapeze artist wanted. Belle Vue Firework Island and Amusement Park.' I'd worked in a circus before, in South Africa: once, when I was eleven, I ran away from my father and stepmother's brutal regime and joined Wilkie's Circus for two months until I was apprehended. I looked back on those days as some of the happiest of my life, when I felt part of an extended family of fairground folk. Now, in 1962, I was seventeen, homeless and needed a job badly, so I rang the number in the advert and arranged an interview.

Speedy Barham was a short, stocky guy with a cheeky grin. He'd been a pilot in the air force but now he owned an aerial circus act that he called the Australian Air Aces. He came forward to greet me in the tent when I arrived, holding out his hand.

'So, you must be Judy.'

'That's me.'

I liked him immediately – he seemed really comfortable with himself, which set me at my ease. I also loved the smell of the place – the bales of hay and animal cages and the lingering sweetness of popcorn and candy floss.

'It's not like a regular job interview, you know,' he grinned. 'Is it OK if you hang around till Thursday?'

'Sure,' I said. I had nowhere else to be.

Speedy put me through my paces for a couple of days. I was skinny, but strong and very determined. I dived right in and hauled equipment, helped to set it up and spent hours swinging upside down on the trapeze as Speedy called out instructions. I made mistakes a couple of times and was terrified he would be cross with me. At home if I got something wrong my father had thought nothing of hurling me across the room, but Speedy just said 'Whoa! I think you'd better try that one again.'

'Don't you feel nervous?' he asked after one session. 'That trapeze is pretty high.'

'It's OK,' I said, but I couldn't really explain to him why I had such steely nerves. The truth was that where I had grown up, getting badly hurt was a certainty. My father beat me almost daily on any pretext. I was used to being covered in bruises. Standing on a swing just didn't hold the same threat, even if I was high up and without a safety harness. I shrugged. Sometimes being on the trapeze took my breath away, but it was no comparison to the kind of terror I had lived with when my father flew off the handle, hurled abuse in my direction and beat me black and blue.

When Speedy offered me the job I was so delighted that my face flushed with happiness. I could feel my cheeks glowing. It was like being accepted into a big happy family – like a dream come true for me. Speedy said I could stay on the fairground site in a 1930s brown coach with a yellow stripe painted all round it, so that solved my accommodation problem. We agreed a wage of eight pounds a week, which was a fortune for a seventeen-year-old in 1962. As Bobby, one of the other aerial artistes, put it 'It's not half as bad as working in Walls' sausage factory.'

The act I was to perform in was an amazing type of aerial acrobatics. Speedy rode a motorbike round a track that was suspended forty feet up in the air. The bike was connected to a narrow platform that see-sawed up and down, causing the bike to somersault through the air with Speedy clinging onto it. Meanwhile, two other girls – Speedy's girlfriend Vicky and Bobby, a glamorous blonde – and I would do a trapeze act above him. At the climax of the act, I had to leave the trapeze and walk slowly along the central platform until my weight caused Speedy's wheels to descend once more onto the track. The show was to be performed outdoors so we'd have to watch out for gusts of wind, or rain making the platform slippery, and everything happened at high speed, without a safety net. There was no margin of error. One lapse of concentration could cost everyone their lives. So when I started we rehearsed the act over and over – it felt like a thousand times.

Speedy was very patient, teaching me how to count between the moves and be very aware of where everyone else was. We rehearsed on the ground first and I got the hang of it quickly. Then we had to get the timing right for Speedy's somersaults.

'I'll call out to you when I'm ready,' he said.

We tried that a couple of times without much success. I'm deaf in my right ear because my eardrum was burst by Dad's girlfriend Freda in one of her vicious attacks when I was just four years old. I couldn't make out Speedy's instructions over the roar of the motorbike.

'I'm sorry,' I said, nervously. No matter how kind everybody seemed I had been brutally tutored to expect a violent reaction if I didn't please. Now I had to come clean about my disability. Fortunately, Speedy was very understanding.

'Don't worry about it, love,' he said. 'There has to be a way round that.' After a bit of thought, he fixed a light to the back of his bike and when he wanted me to move, he switched the light on. It was a signal I could easily follow.

I was incredibly grateful – I couldn't quite believe that everyone was being so nice to me, something I just wasn't used to at all.

Gradually we started rehearsing the more dangerous tricks high up on the equipment and before I knew it Speedy announced that we were ready to face the public.

Belle Vue's Firework Island was an enormous entertainment complex, and huge audiences were normal at the shows. The first night I listened to the crowd arriving and peeked out from the bus where we were getting ready. Everyone was laughing and joking, staring towards the island with anticipation. The atmosphere was fantastic. Now I realized I had to prove that I could hold my nerve in front of an audience. I pulled on a leotard I'd been given, slapped on a bit of stage makeup and tied my dark hair back in a ponytail.

As we came out the crowd were cheering like crazy. I got a tingly feeling of excitement as I looked up at the rig. Speedy went first to get himself ready on the bike, then Bobby and Vicky climbed to their stations while I got into place. The faces of the audience turned towards us as we moved higher and higher and I could feel the tension mounting as the crowd grew quiet. It was obvious how dangerous the act was – just being so high up without a safety net was risky.

Vicky gave the thumbs up once we were all in place then Speedy got on the bike and began to ride. From that moment on, I shut out the audience and just counted carefully. Because we had rehearsed as much as we had, it meant that I hardly had to think. I span on the trapeze for ten counts and then I had six seconds until my next move. At just the right moment, I let go and dropped upside down, catching the bar with my feet and spreading my arms like an eagle over Speedy's head as he zoomed past. A surge of excitement coursed through my whole body – an adrenaline rush that comes with flinging yourself into a dive, and having time stand still until you know you're safe. Then as I surfaced into real time again, I caught the reaction of the audience. Everyone was clapping and cheering and I felt exhilarated from the rush of the dive and then the thrill of having everyone applauding me. A smile crept across my face and I couldn't have wiped it off if I'd tried. As I moved carefully along the platform to lower Speedy, who was still somersaulting with the bike, I knew that all the hard work was more than worthwhile. The crowd went wild again and my face glowed with satisfaction.

'This is it!' I thought. 'I can't believe that I get to do this every day!'

After that first performance I felt so proud of myself. I was the youngest on the team by miles and I had done it. The show left me on a high. In fact, I was dying to get out there and do it all again. The others were more experienced and consequently calmer so I tried not to show just how excited I was.

'That was fine,' Speedy said thoughtfully. 'I think we can go on tour now. I'll see if I can get some dates organized.'

I hadn't realized that we'd get to go away as well. 'Where will we tour to?' I asked keenly.

'I'll see what I can line up. Just round the country a bit. Anything within a day's drive.'

I told them that I had no ties at all, nothing keeping me in the Manchester area. I could travel anywhere they wanted me to, round the world if need be.

Every few weeks Speedy got a booking and the four of us would set off in the bus, with our gear packed into the boot or tied onto the roof. Travelling around was hard work because of all the setting up that had to be done – I don't think I've ever been quite so exhausted. On top of hauling the equipment we performed in two shows a day. But it was fun and I loved it. I wouldn't have swapped my job for anything.

It was sunny that summer and we drove with the bus door open. I loved sitting in the breeze on the steps with the road whizzing by below me. Of course, these days the police would go crazy about that kind of thing.

'You better not fall asleep there, Judy,' Speedy teased. 'We don't want to lose you!'

Actually, a couple of times it was a close thing.

'I'll be fine,' I said. 'You just worry about the driving.'

Most people at the fair had more than one act and it wasn't long before I was asked to expand my repertoire. On top of the Australian Air Aces, Speedy was a knife thrower and shooter and Vicky was his target. She wore a green, spangly bikini with cowboy fringes on it. I agreed to fill in for her sometimes.

'Don't worry,' she told me. 'It's only gone wrong once.' She showed me a three-inch scar on her arm where Speedy's aim had gone awry. 'That was a while ago,' she said. 'He's much more experienced now. The main thing is to stay absolutely still.'

I swallowed nervously and tried not to think too much.

Speedy set up the board he used as a backdrop and winked at me as I climbed onto the podium and took my place. As I stood there waiting for the first of the razor-sharp blades, all I could think was, 'I hope he doesn't miss!'

Speedy lined up and threw the first knife fast, with deadly accuracy. A bead of sweat trickled slowly down my forehead as every sense in my body came alive. I couldn't see it but I heard the blade whizzing past me and embedding itself in the cork backdrop with a thump. My instincts were bristling. My father had thrown things at me all the time. Anything he could lay his hands on, in fact. I had learned to watch the path of the object as it whizzed towards me and move quickly out of the way. The difficulty here was to trust Speedy and stay absolutely still. I heard the second knife whoosh past and land deep in the cork on the other side of my head. Time seemed to stop. I realized that if I was going to hold the position I just had to block it out. The third knife landed in between my legs and I focused hard on my breathing.

'Stay still,' I willed myself. As far as I was concerned this was a test of my courage and I wasn't going to chicken out now as, one after the other, I was circled by the blades.

'You're a cool one,' Speedy said with a grin at the end.

'Thanks.' My skin was clammy with sweat and I could feel the adrenaline pumping round my body as I stepped away from the outline of knives behind me. I'd done it.

'Fancy trying the revolver, then?' he asked.

'OK. Why not?' I think in some ways I was always looking for challenges to stretch me a bit and test my own
strength. If Speedy had asked me to walk on a tightrope
over Niagara Falls, I'd have done it just to prove that I
could.

Vicky helped me into a tunic that had balloons attached
to it. I took up my position again and Speedy tied a blindfold round his eyes and began to shoot at the balloons. The
gun shots were very loud and came in quick succession. I
did my best to stay calm. As the balloons burst one by one,
my tunic fell to the ground, revealing me in a sequinned
bikini. Though my heart was thumping I lifted up my
hands and gestured triumphantly as I'd seen Vicky do.
Then I took a bow to an imaginary audience and Speedy
jumped up beside me and bowed too.

'Well done, Judy,' Speedy said. 'It's as though you were
born to it.'

Little did he know.

The audience loved that act. Speedy was so reliable that I
came to trust him completely. I loved the act and felt great-
ly honoured when asked to fill in for Vicky. Their belief in
me gave me a real feeling of acceptance.

After the show Bobby often went out on dates with boys
she'd met, but I stayed behind on the bus. I hadn't a clue
about romance. At the age of seventeen, most people know
about physical attraction and dating but I was emotionally
stunted by my early life. I guess the fact I was so young
made them feel protective because Speedy and Vicky took
me under their wing and kept an eye on me during those
first idyllic weeks of my new job.

The easy happiness wasn't to last, though. A new challenge was about to come into my life, one that I had absolutely no resources at all for dealing with. His name was Roger Lethbridge.

## Chapter Two

One day when we got back to Belle Vue after a week of touring, Speedy asked me if I'd be interested in another job.

'You'd be working with the boys in a different act of mine,' he explained. 'It used to be called The Hell Drivers, but I renamed it. Now it's The Globe of Death.'

'What?' I asked. 'Like The Wall of Death?'

Speedy shrugged his shoulders nonchalantly. 'Nah,' he said, 'The Wall of Death is easy. You just ride a bike up a wall. This is much more interesting. Come and have a look.'

The Globe was a spherical wire mesh cage, about sixteen feet in diameter, with an entrance on one side. Speedy explained that the boys drove a motorbike round the inside and I was incredulous at first. How was that possible?

'Roger!' he shouted. 'Come and show Judy, would you?'

Roger emerged pushing a black motorbike. He was more or less my age, dressed in leather trousers and a jacket. He had still, blue eyes and seemed very confident. I thought he looked nice.

'Hi,' he smiled and he pulled on his helmet.

I nodded back.

Inside the Globe, Roger began to ride in low circles, then as he built up momentum he zoomed upside down over the top.

'Wow!' I was gobsmacked. This guy was an amazing rider.

'It gets better,' said Speedy, like a gleeful kid. 'We got two bikes.'

The second rider, Noggi, had to go in the opposite direction from Roger. It was another split-second timing stunt as the bikes missed each other by a fraction of a second on each revolution. I watched as Noggi came out and Roger and he started the act again, this time together. In seconds they were zooming around the inside of the cage, running loops past each other, upside down. I could see the act was very, very dangerous.

'So what do you want me to do, Speedy?'

'You, love, are going to go-go dance right in the middle and let them ride round you.' Speedy nodded to himself. 'Crowd puller.'

It looked like a bit of fun. There wasn't any skill in it, after all. I just had to stand there and keep my nerve. I was always up for that kind of challenge.

'Sure,' I said. 'No problem.'

Noggi and Roger stopped in the base of the Globe and pulled off their motorcycle helmets. I climbed in and stood on the metal base plate in the centre. Speedy demonstrated what he wanted me to do, waving his thick arms in the air, then the boys put their helmets back on and began to ride around the base just as before. I could feel the wind whistling past me as they built up speed. I lifted my arms and began to dance on the spot, just ignoring the bikes as they flew by. Close up I realized exactly how fast they had to ride in order to circle upside down inside the cage. It was noisy in there and the air was full of petrol fumes that caught in my throat. I held my ground and danced on the marked spot. After a few minutes the boys made it back down to the bottom, one on either side of me, the engines still fired up.

'Good one,' Roger said and gave me a smile.

So I was in. During the days we rehearsed and carted the equipment to and from the garage shed while maintenance and repairs were done. Sometimes we had costume fittings to do. Vicky could whiz up stunning new costumes at the speed of light, and I let her make all the decisions for me because she knew what colours worked best under the lights. When she measured me, she sighed, jealous of my twenty-four-inch waist and skinny figure.

That summer the Globe really caught the public's imagination and Speedy had a big hit on his hands. The local papers came to Belle Vue and took photographs of Roger, Noggi and me standing at the front of the cage, sitting on the bikes, and then posing inside with the bikes' engines started up.

'Smile,' the photographer said. 'You're going to be a pin-up girl!'

The truth was that I had no notion of myself that way. I'd always avoided being the centre of attention so the thought of being a pin-up girl made me very uncomfortable.

'Not me,' I mumbled shyly, staring at the ground.

At night I slept in the compound on my own because everyone else had homes to go to. I loved it there by myself in the dark. There were high walls all around and the gates were closed and locked. It seemed really quiet in contrast to the rest of the day, which was filled with hurdy-gurdy music and the chattering of the crowd, punctuated by the screams and gasps of the audience during performances. Once everyone had gone the only noise was the animals in their cages – marsupials, bears, horses, dogs – and that was about it. I sat out on the steps to look at the moon and drank a cup of cocoa as I listened to the odd growl or bark or whinny. I was at peace.

One evening I was hovering in the shadows beside the bus, peeking at the last of the audience as they made their way out at closing time. The stalls were almost empty and it was late. I had done all my chores and everything was put away. I was still wearing one of my showgirl costumes with a big, brown coat pulled over the top because the nights had started to get chilly.

Suddenly Roger appeared. He hesitated for a moment and then came to join me. I was always glad to have a chat with Roger. It was a nice time of night to have a chinwag about everything that had gone on during the day.

'They're in right high spirits tonight,' he said, lighting up a Senior Service and flicking the match onto the ground. 'There was a guy down in Paddock Wood last year got his timing wrong with a motorbike stunt. I heard he lost his leg.'

'We took the Aces to Paddock Wood,' I said. 'A couple of months ago.'

Roger took a deep draw on his cigarette. We waved to Bobby who was leaving with a couple of her friends. The public were almost completely gone.

'Nice night,' he said.

Then a couple stopped only a few feet away from us. They couldn't have noticed we were there. The girl was carrying a teddy bear, which they'd won on one of the stalls. Roger and I instinctively stayed hidden in the shadows. He turned his cigarette into the palm of his hand. Suddenly the man reached out and kissed his girlfriend passionately. She laughed and they walked off.

Roger had a grin on his face. 'Wonder where they're off to?'

I shrugged my shoulders. I didn't have any curiosity about those things at all. The couple might as well have come from another planet. I'd never had a boyfriend or felt any urge to get myself one. That was something other people did – not me.

'Maybe they're going dancing,' Roger suggested. 'Do you like dancing, Judy?'

'Yeah. I suppose.' I had never been to a proper dance.

'Well, we should go some time,' Roger stubbed out his cigarette. 'It'd be a laugh.' He walked off after the couple, in the direction of the gates. Then he turned.

'Saturday night,' he said. 'I'll come and get you.'

I was pleased. I loved music and going dancing would be a first for me. It may sound strange but I was so naïve that it genuinely didn't occur to me that Roger might see this as a date in a romantic sense. I felt like such an outsider that I was just surprised to find someone who actually wanted to spend time with me. Roger seemed nice – and, as he'd said, it was only a bit of fun.

# Chapter Three

Speedy had never said that I shouldn't go out on the town after hours – we'd never discussed it – but still, it felt mischievous. This would be my first time out in Manchester at night. On the Saturday of the dance, Roger borrowed a long ladder to get me out of the locked compound, as if I was escaping from prison. We arranged to meet at the wall beside the horseboxes at nine o'clock.

'You there, Judy?' he called over.

'Yeah.'

I heard him position the ladder against the wall and a few seconds later his face appeared at the top. Then he hauled himself up to a sitting position, pulled the ladder over and motioned for me to climb up towards him. 'I'm a right minx now,' I thought to myself, looking over my shoulder as if someone might be watching. But there was nobody there. I launched myself at the ladder, thinking, 'This is going to be a laugh.'

I scaled the wall and sat on top next to him.

'Nice up here,' he said and climbed down the other side ahead of me.

We hid the ladder in the scrubland like escapees and headed off to the Belle Vue Ballroom.

It was dark by the time we arrived and the dance hall was very busy. Everyone seemed so glamorous and in-the-know. I'd worn my only dress – a red and white check with scoop neck and a wide, red belt – and I had my hair tied back. Some of the women looked amazing with sparkling jewellery, high heels and beautiful make-up. I caught a whiff of perfume as they passed. Roger had dressed up too. He looked really smart in his shirt and trousers.

'Come on,' he said, grabbing my hand and pulling me onto the dance floor.

The band was playing the Twist and everyone was dancing full pelt, gyrating like crazy. We flung ourselves into the crowd and joined in. It was fantastic. I loved dancing like that, losing myself in the music without any of my normal self-consciousness. As a kid I had always loved classical music but the Twist was fun and it was an amazing feeling to be part of the crowd with everyone dancing together. Because of the way I'd grown up I always felt separate to other people as if I was a different species entirely. Dancing like this was an incredible experience for me because it was something normal that I could join in and feel part of.

Up at the bar there was so much to look at – the rows of bottles and the waiters with their bow ties and all the people, chattering and excited and dressed up. Roger got me a tomato juice then we leaned against the bar and talked for ages. He told me he had lived in Manchester all his life and came from a big, close family – the eldest of ten kids. I lapped up his stories of an idyllic childhood playing in the street and going to the local school. Then he started talking about motorbikes. Like lots of young guys, Roger was fascinated by bikes. He was a great stunt rider though he said what he really liked best was driving on the open road. Fast.

'I like it when we're touring in the bus,' I told him. 'I sit on the steps and watch the road whiz past.'

'Yeah,' he said 'that's it exactly. Open to the road.' He finished his pint.

'Come on, Judy,' he said. 'Let's get back to the floor.'

I couldn't wait and eagerly followed him so we could join the crowd once more. It wasn't long before we were pink-cheeked and out of breath with the best of them. It was exhilarating, a real high for me.

Walking away from the ballroom at the end of the night Roger lit a cigarette. The stars were out. I hummed a couple of the dance tunes and he caught my hand and twirled me round.

'That was amazing!' I exclaimed.

Roger took a deep draw of his cigarette and regarded me closely. 'You're all right, Judy,' he said.

We ran the last hundred yards or so and grabbed the ladder from its hiding place, propping it up against the wall. I had had a good time, but I wasn't sure what to say to Roger now we were on our own. I felt slightly awkward. Relating to other people was difficult for me because I had had no role models. Now the night was over I felt slightly out of my depth.

'Thanks,' I mumbled and scuttled up the ladder.

'You want to pull it over? I can come up and help,' Roger offered.

'No. I can jump from here. It's fine.'

He gave me a wave and walked off with the ladder over his shoulder, the glowing ember of the cigarette bobbing along beside him.

After that night at the Belle Vue Ballroom, Roger took an interest in me. Sometimes when I came off stage from an Australian Air Aces performance he'd be waiting outside the bus for me, and sometimes he helped me when I was moving the gear. Unlike Bobby, I hadn't a clue about the rules of the game and I still thought he was just being friendly.

When Speedy announced we were touring to Southampton, Roger surprised me by going in a sulk. 'You'll be up to all sorts down there,' he said gloomily.

'What do you mean?' I had no idea what he was on about, but he didn't enlighten me – just stomped around in a mood.

He came to wave us off the night we left and said 'Have a nice time,' but his voice didn't sound very cheerful.

'If I can't be good, I'll definitely be careful,' Bobby joked and Roger glowered at her. We waved at him from the window as we drove off.

I enjoyed Southampton. Vicky and I went to see the boats in the dock and watched as a huge liner came in. The shows went really well and at night I fell asleep listening to the horns of the ships on the Sound.

A week later, after a run of shows, Roger was waiting when we got back after the long drive north. He was standing in the space right beside where the bus parked and he had a face like fizz.

'What the hell happened to you?' he demanded. He seemed really upset.

'What do you mean?'

'You could have called, you know. I was worried.'

'But you knew where I was,' I said, astonished. It had never occurred to me to call. No-one had ever cared where I was. When I moved to Belle Vue, my mother didn't even ask where I was going to be staying.

'What did you do?' Roger quizzed me.

'You know what I did. We did the show.'

'And after?'

'Had something to eat. We had showers over at this house. Speedy organized it. I went for a bath two nights.'

Roger had a tortured expression on his face. 'I bet Bobby went out.'

'Yes.'

'With men?'

'Yes.'

'But not you?'

'No.'

'Are you sure?'

I thought that Roger caring about where I was and what I was up to was sweet. I didn't mind at all. I'd seen Bobby playing one guy off against another and making herself tantalizingly unavailable but that kind of thing was in a different league. I was extremely naïve. I don't think Roger ever realized that.

'Next tour you have to ring me every day,' he insisted.

'OK,' I said. 'If you like.'

A couple of weeks later Speedy organized a few days at Paddock Wood in Kent. We'd been there before and I liked it. There was a phone box just up the road and I made sure I had lots of change so I could call Roger. When I rang him in the evening he quizzed me about every second of my day and sulked when I told him that Bobby had gone out with a couple of guys after the show.

'And what did you do?'

'Nothing.'

'What are you going to do now?'

'Go back to the bus to bed.'

He didn't believe me. 'You're staying in on your own?' he asked in disbelief.

'Yes.'

No matter how much I tried to reassure him, he never seemed satisfied and I simply felt confused. I was desperately trying to figure out what was going on. I knew he must like me. We spent a lot of time together; surely he wouldn't do that if he didn't enjoy my company? So why was he quizzing me like this? I concluded that he must care about me and that in some way, I was doing something wrong. 'I must try harder to please him,' I decided. There was something about it all that felt forbidden and dangerous. I knew I was out of my depth, but I couldn't quite put a finger on it.

When we got back to Belle Vue after that run, I went to find Roger. He was polishing his bike but as soon as he saw me he leapt up and pulled me towards him, wrapping his arms tightly around me. No one had ever hugged me that way before and my eyes welled up with tears. I could hear my heart pounding. It was a very powerful feeling, being surrounded by him and held like that. In the past if anyone had got that close to me it meant things were about to turn violent. By contrast Roger's arms felt tender.

'I missed you so much,' he said and he kissed me.

My knees almost gave way and I kissed him back and put my arms around his waist. There was no room for any doubts. I felt completely engulfed. This was something very private and very beautiful.

Roger drew back. 'I'm glad you're home,' he said with a grin and I couldn't stop smiling either.

A few minutes later I was watching the show from the sidelines. Roger was practically fearless and very, very accurate. You had to admire his riding skills. When the show had finished and the audience were clapping, he looked over to me and he winked. I had never felt so special.

'So is this it?' I thought to myself. 'Is this what everyone goes on about, what all the pop songs are written about? I suppose this must be what love is.'

# Chapter Four

*A*fter that Roger took me with him almost everywhere he went. I couldn't quite believe that I had a boyfriend. I felt like an actress playing a part. But this, I told myself, is what it must be like to be normal. It seemed very abstract, like a strange kind of dream.

Roger was handsome and we had a lot in common. We both enjoyed the atmosphere at Belle Vue and shared the excitement of being daredevils. Most of the time we nipped off and went on a ride if we had a spare hour here or there. We didn't ride on the rollercoaster – none of the fairground people ever did – because the maintenance guys told us it wasn't sound and there had been some horrible accidents.

Instead we rode the dodgems, the caterpillar ride or the carousel. Sometimes we'd pop in and see friends on other shows – such as Kiki and Pepe, who had a children's zoo with miniature, black poodles that were trained to have picnics or push each other around in a toy pram.

This kind of easy acceptance was a dream to me. Sleeping on the cold floor of a shack in an alleyway when I was homeless I used to make up stories about falling in love, having a family and being married with kids of my own. It kept me going through the long, cold, sleepless nights when I was shivering and ravenous. If I hadn't eaten for days I'd imagine sitting down to a family meal or even serving up food to my own children. The raw material for these fantasies came from films that I had sneaked into at the drive-in movies. I particularly loved *Three Coins in a Fountain* and *Mardi Gras* with Pat Boone. The stories I conjured up were about a perfect life in which everything worked out for me.

Now, with Roger, at least some of these fantasies seemed to be coming true. When he kissed me I felt almost completely overwhelmed and when we went away touring, I couldn't wait to get back to see him again. But it wasn't quite as rosy as the Hollywood-tinged storylines that had brightened the dark midnight hours when I was sleeping rough. The way he spoke to me sometimes made me feel totally inadequate, as though I wasn't as good as him, but I always thought this was my fault because I felt so separate from everything and everyone. Intimacy of all kinds was completely new and I blamed myself for not managing to make things truly perfect.

One Sunday Roger took me out on a surprise date after the afternoon performance. I had no idea where we were going and he refused to tell me. We took a bus to the suburbs and on the way Roger eyed my outfit critically, adjusting the collar of my blouse. A few minutes later we got off in Wythenshawe. Without saying a word, Roger turned down a street and I followed obediently. He stopped outside a brick council house and stubbed out his cigarette.

'Right,' he said, taking me by the hand.

I had no idea what I was walking into.

Inside, his whole family was assembled for a meal. The room was chock-a-block. My life so far had been almost entirely solitary and I couldn't have imagined so many people living together in such close quarters. All nine of his siblings were there that day. Roger's mother, a tiny woman with lively eyes, invited me in.

'Hello Judy,' she said, looking me up and down. 'Roger has told us all about you.'

Roger stared at his feet and I suddenly worried that I might not measure up. I wished I had had a chance to prepare. Then his father came over. He was a beanpole of a man and must have towered at least a foot over his wife.

'Hello, Mr Lethbridge. Nice to meet you,' I shook his hand.

There were kids everywhere in that house. It was a lot to take in all at once, especially with all the noise going on. Everyone talked at the same time. The younger ones were playing on the floor and a squabble had broken out which Mrs Lethbridge silenced with one fiery glance.

'I'll never remember all these names,' I panicked and just kept smiling. I'd never been to a family dinner before and had no idea what was expected of me. Was I supposed to initiate conversation by asking polite questions? Shyly, I decided that I would just speak when spoken to.

Peter, one of Roger's brothers, asked which act I was in.

'The Australian Air Aces,' I began, enthusiastically.

'I fancy Roger's job,' Peter interrupted.

'You'll get a proper job when the time comes,' Mr Lethbridge spat at him. It was clear they had had this conversation before.

'My job *is* a proper job, Dad,' Roger objected. 'The pay is good. You can't earn a weekly paypacket like mine down the factory.'

But Mr Lethbridge clearly didn't approve of his son's choices or want another of his children involved in the amusement park.

'So, Judy, where are your family?' Mrs Lethbridge asked as we sat down at the table.

'Judy's a dark horse. She won't tell me anything about them,' Roger butted in.

The truth was that I didn't know what I could possibly say. Roger had asked me about my family several times but I had spent my whole life keeping silent about the things that had gone on in my childhood. Saying anything would have meant opening up emotionally in a way that I just wasn't capable of doing.

'I don't have much family,' I started. I suppose I should have thought up some kind of cover story, but I'd never been any good at lying. I noticed a couple of the younger girls staring at me – not having family must have seemed peculiar to them. Mrs Lethbridge looked at me for a second and then started to serve the food. I felt her eyes on me right through the meal and I knew what she was thinking. What kind of a girl runs away to the fair and doesn't have a family? It didn't seem respectable.

I was never at ease in that house but at the time I blamed myself. It was nice of Roger to bring me home with him and I was fascinated by the normality of it all. Was this what family life was really about? Mr Lethbridge being tough on Peter while Mrs Lethbridge ruled the roost with the younger kids. I didn't have anything real to compare it with though the atmosphere was certainly worlds away from my childhood fantasies of happy family life.

That summer Roger's sister Jean turned nineteen and I was invited along to the celebration dinner in a restaurant.

Jean was glamorous and confident, and it was strange to think that she and I were almost the same age (I had turned eighteen now) because in every other way we were poles apart. I felt self-conscious throughout the meal and didn't utter a single word all night. There was such a crowd of them and I desperately wanted to feel comfortable enough to join in, but I couldn't. I'd had to learn how to survive for the whole of my life, alone. I was very streetwise and canny, but emotionally I was nothing more than a naïve child.

One night at the Globe, after we had taken our bows and the audience was leaving, Roger caught my hand briefly.

'Judy,' he started. 'You shouldn't have to work like this.'

I was puzzled. I loved working.

'It's dangerous,' he continued. 'You risk your life every time you get on stage. I don't want that for you. I want to look after you,' he said. 'I want you to be with me.'

This was all very odd. Roger fumbled in his pocket and pulled out a little diamond ring. It flashed in the lights. 'Will you marry me?' he asked.

I was stunned. Roger wanted to be married to me. I slowly ran through everything I thought that meant. I imagined our home. I pictured a place full of love and security like those I had seen in the movies. For me, this was a dream greater than any other. Roger wanted to live with me.

'You want us to have a home together?'

He nodded. 'Think about it,' he said. 'We can talk about it later.'

After the final show we went for a meal. There was a restaurant down the road that was open late. As we walked in I suddenly felt very special. Roger ordered for both of us

– some ham and potatoes. I could see he was nervous. I had no nerves at all – I just felt excited. Was this really happening to me? To little, skinny Judy with the scruffy hair? Judy whom no one had ever loved? Judy with no family and no proper home?

'Did you have a think about it?' Roger asked.

I hesitated, shyly.

'I want you to be mine,' he said. 'That's what it is. I love you, Judy.'

I looked up at him. There were tears in my eyes. His words sent floods of emotions coursing through me that I couldn't understand. I just wanted to feel like this forever and to give him my whole soul.

'Yes. I'll marry you,' I said.

And we were both laughing all of a sudden.

'Mrs Roger Lethbridge. I'm going to be Mrs Roger Lethbridge,' I thought to myself as if in a dream.

Roger was twenty-one the following month and when he told his family that we were getting married his mother insisted on organizing the wedding. She had already made a booking for his birthday party and the whole wedding celebration just became an extension of that. Speedy had organized a lot of touring for us during that month and I came back from a few days away to find that the wedding flowers had been organized, the invitations sent out and a few dresses set aside for me to try. It was like being carried along on a tidal wave.

Normally the bride's father pays for weddings but, given the circumstances with my family, Mrs Lethbridge was paying for everything. I wondered whether I should invite my Mum and sisters, but I didn't like to add to the cost of everything and I couldn't imagine how I would have introduced them. Anyway, I'm pretty sure they wouldn't have come.

Sometimes, late at night as I lay down to sleep on the bus, I did wonder if this was right for me but I had no way of telling and no one I could turn to for advice. I couldn't talk to Bobby or Vicky because I didn't know how to put into words what I was feeling, and didn't want to be disloyal to Roger. Besides, the wedding was his 21st birthday celebration and I couldn't spoil that for him. I had doubts nipping at my heels – just little things. Sometimes he would interrupt or undermine me in public in a way that felt quite rude to me. Sometimes he was critical and made me feel inferior, but I had no way of knowing that these things weren't part of a normal loving relationship so I tried to kick my doubts away. I liked Roger. Everyone was being so kind. 'It'll all work out,' I told myself.

One day a minister friend of Vicky's came to the amusement park. I was worried because I thought that I might need to get permission to get married. If you were under twenty-one that was normal, so I plucked up the courage to ask this man. He was quite serious but he had a kind face and he was older, which made me feel secure.

'I was abandoned by my parents,' I explained. 'My mother doesn't want anything to do with me and my father is in South Africa. He never wanted to look after me. Do you think that I can still marry Roger? Do I need to get parental permission?'

'Well, you are only eighteen,' he said kindly, 'but this is a unique situation. Let me look into it for you.'

A couple of days later he came back and said that everything would be fine. I remember wishing that I could ask him for more advice, but I couldn't quite think how to frame the unformed question that was hovering in my mind. It felt so disloyal. These doubts surely were about my own inadequacies. Here it was – everything I had ever dreamed of. I pinned my hopes on that.

When I walked down the aisle at St Luke's Church in Wythenshawe in November 1963, I wore white. Mrs Lethbridge had done a good job – everything ran like clockwork. Most of all, my heart was full of hope. I believed I was walking into a world full of love. I thought things were going to be perfect.

'Do you promise to love, honour and obey?' the minister asked and I took that question very seriously.

'I do,' I said firmly.

I felt wonderful that day. But within days after the wedding I realized that Roger had a very different kind of life in mind – and love had nothing to do with it.

# Chapter Five

*A*fter the wedding party was over, there was no honey-moon. Roger and I moved to a small brick house opposite his Grandad's place in Compass Street, Openshawe, and everything changed completely. We didn't have marital relations that first night because he was too drunk but on the second night of married life he insisted. For some reason, I hadn't made the connection between marriage and sex but now I realized I'd just have to put up with it. It was extremely hard for me because I had been raped twice as a child: once on a beach on the Isle of Man when I was eight when Freda and Dad had left me on my own all day; and then again when I was twelve and sleeping rough in an alleyway in Johannesburg. I hadn't told Roger about those occasions but he must have been able to see how nervous I was about going to bed with him.

As soon as our marriage was consummated, everything changed. Roger made it clear he considered himself the master of the house and as far as he was concerned it was his job to keep me in line. From the moment we first walked through the front door into the small, dark rooms inside, I sensed a difference in my new husband. He was no longer loving or warm towards me. When people realize that you've got no one behind you and nowhere to run, they can become very manipulative and controlling. I was his chattel, his possession. He'd made me give up the job at Belle Vue so now he controlled the purse strings and he was determined I was going to earn my keep. Overnight, my time at the circus became a distant dream and the run-up to the wedding and our courtship days seemed like an impossible fairy tale. I was back in a position of being abused, but at least I knew how to deal with that. It's what I had grown up with after all.

I tried to be positive. There was some furniture that had been left by the previous tenants but it was pretty sparse, and that was all we had, along with a frying pan, a pot, two plates and two sets of cutlery. That didn't matter to me though. As I explored the place for the first time I was sure that I could turn it into a home.

I missed the excitement and glamour of the circus but that wasn't where my duty lay now. I wanted to be there with a meal when Roger got home. I wanted to be the loving homemaker, a good wife, cooking and washing and doing all the things that I'd always dreamed about. It even crossed my mind that I would love to have a child. I knew things didn't have to be the way they had been when I was growing up. I wanted everything to be different and I was determined to do my best.

However, I didn't realize then that my best would never be good enough for Roger. From that first moment the house on Compass Street became a prison and Roger was my brutal jailer. Life became a series of rules that he dictated and the punishment for coming up short was extreme.

\* \* \*

We hardly ever went out. The lazy days of wandering around the rides at Belle Vue were gone and Roger relentlessly bullied me and told me how worthless I was. He wanted to control me completely yet when I let him take charge he seemed to despise me for it. It was as if, having married him, I had lost everything.

'You are disgusting,' Roger raged. 'Why would I want to take you anywhere?'

If I started a conversation or voiced an opinion he would cut in immediately. 'You have nothing of importance to say, Judy, so shut up.'

It quickly became clear that Roger had a temper as foul as my father's and that the consequences of not following his orders were a beating that was all too familiar. It may sound strange but I can't even remember the first time he hit me. If you came from a decent family where you hadn't ever been beaten up, I'm sure your husband hitting you would come as a huge shock, but I just accepted it. I believed that's how relationships were. I remember Freda once saying to me, 'You go to the ends of the earth for your husband,' and I'd witnessed at first hand all the abuse she took from Dad. So this is how it was going to be. If I just tried harder, surely I'd get things right and then Roger wouldn't have any reason to hit me?

Each morning I had to rise early and make breakfast. Roger insisted on having this in bed. I was to make fried eggs on toast perfectly to his specification. The eggs had to be whole and the yolks had to have a white surface, no yellow showing. I was terrified of those eggs breaking in the frying pan not least because I didn't have much money to buy food. If the eggs were broken Roger would attack me and make me cook more, and then if there were no more left God knows what he might do. The toast also had to be just the way he liked it. No burnt bits whatsoever. There were many times when one way or another the breakfast was unacceptable and it was hurled at me viciously, hot tea and all.

After breakfast, Roger's clothes had to be laid out in a particular way for the morning and once he'd finished eating I was expected to dress him. This was a daily ritual and he would not get up for work until I had performed it. All the while he criticized and mocked me, telling me how useless I was. I tried to keep silent and not provoke him in any way but that wasn't always possible. If Roger was in a bad mood then there was nothing I could do.

'You useless bitch!' he screamed when I dropped a cup one morning, and he lunged to grab my hair and hit me round the face, back and forwards, over and over again. 'Do you think I'm made of money?' Close-up his eyes glowed with hatred, just like the devil eyes my father used to have when he beat me senseless as a little girl. I'd feel his hot breath and drops of spittle on my cheek and I became as passive as I could, not even raising my hands to protect myself, just waiting for the rage to diminish. As a child, I had learned not to answer back, not to struggle, and now I reverted to the same behaviour.

I was horrified to find that I had married a man with remarkable similarities to my father but at the same time I had the sinking feeling that it must be my own fault. If only I could manage things properly then surely Roger would be pleased with me. I wanted to turn things around, to go back to something like the relationship we had before we were married. I desperately believed it was possible but no matter what I did Roger was relentlessly suspicious of my motives. I sat downstairs, bewildered, for days on end, completely alone apart from my husband's vicious company, going over the vow I had made in Church. I had promised to obey and that's what I had to do.

Then there was the daily round of endless accusations. When Roger got home he'd want to know where I had been, who I had spoken to, and who had been to the door. He forbade me from going to the shops alone; nor was I allowed on a bus by myself but had to wait until he was able to accompany me. If I wanted to go out I needed his permission. He accused me of having affairs behind his back, and told me that I was nothing but a whore who slept around. I remembered the questions he'd asked me when I used to go touring and how jealous he'd seemed and I realized that this was the same feeling that had now escalated out of control. I remembered how he'd once made a comment about a dress I'd worn or how he'd browbeaten me a couple of times to tell him about my family or spoken over me when we were out for dinner. These were the early shadows of more extreme behaviour, and I couldn't understand how it had got so out of hand. Still he was my husband, he was bigger and stronger than I was and the truth was I had nowhere to go. If I ran away to the circus, after all, Roger would already be there.

'If you ever leave me, I'll come and get you,' he threatened. 'If you leave me, I'll bloody kill you.'

I knew he meant it. I felt trapped and instead of making an escape plan I determined to fix it by being better at everything I did. If only I could be a good-enough wife, everything would be fine.

\* \* \*

One day, when I'd still only been married a couple of weeks, I took our washing to the laundrette. Roger had said this was all right. 'You're a scrubber anyway,' he sniped.

At that time no one did laundry at home. I packed all our dirty stuff into two big carrier bags and set off down the road. When I got there it was busy. Women were standing round chatting as they waited for their loads to finish. Up at the back there was a kettle and someone had made a pot of tea. I got in the queue.

It was certainly better than when I was growing up and I used to have to go to the washhouse with Freda. Even when I was under school age she made me haul a heavy steel bath full of laundry for her. Washing the linen would take her all day. In Openshawe, where Roger and I lived, there was a brand new laundry with big, steel machines. You just had to wait for the machine to do your washing and then transfer your load into one of the driers.

In front of me there was a cheery woman who was sorting out masses of kids clothes.

'Looks like you've got quite a brood there,' I said.

'Yes,' she smiled. 'Keeps you busy. How about you?' she glanced over at the contents of my bag.

'No. Just married a fortnight ago,' I said, trying to smile bravely.

'Oh that's a good time of your life. You savour it, love. I'm Kathleen McAvoy.'

I shook her hand. 'Judy Lethbridge.' My married name still sounded foreign when I said it.

'Well, Mrs Lethbridge,' she said, 'it's nice to meet you.'

Kathleen helped me operate the machines and showed me how much washing powder to use. She told me about her sons, Brian, Gary and Mark. Mark, the youngest, had only just started school. The older boys, she said, were wild.

'They're good kids though. Mind you, the noise sometimes! Still, it's lonely round the house without the little one there,' Kathleen said. 'But you never know. I hope I'll have a little girl next. What are you planning?'

I shrugged my shoulders.

'Oh,' she laughed, as if that explained my reticence. 'Newly wed. I forgot.'

Once the washing was all done Kathleen and I left the laundrette together and wandered back up towards Compass Street. I told her about my time at Belle Vue and it turned out she had come to see the show a few months before with her cousin.

'Ron stayed in with the kids for once. Was that you on the trapeze? I can't believe it. Lord, you must miss that, love.'

'Do you fancy coming in for a cup of tea?' I asked.

'Aye,' she said. 'That'd be nice.'

I put the key in the lock and we left our laundry bags in the hallway.

'Nice for you and your husband to be just starting out together.' Kathleen took in the sparse surroundings as I put on the kettle. I made a pot of tea and put it on the kitchen table to brew. I was just about to pour it when I heard the key in the front door.

'That'll be Roger,' I said, and immediately anxiety filled the pit of my stomach. It was too early for him to come back. There shouldn't be a problem, I told myself. I'll just introduce Kathleen to him. It'll be fine. She's a neighbour. But one look at Roger's face and it was clear he was furious.

'What the hell is this? A tea party?' he spat at me.

Kathleen got up uncomfortably. 'I'll just pop off then, shall I?'

'Just pop off then, shall I?' Roger mimicked her and then turned his wrath on me. 'Swanning round all day with your mates, are you? Doing whatever you want? Enjoying yourself, are you? This is my house, you know.'

I could see he was building up to a real fury. He looked as if he might smash something.

'You're my wife!' he shouted. 'Mine! And you go bringing people back to my house without my permission. Jesus! You're so two-faced. I never know what the hell you're up to.'

Kathleen started to make for the door.

'I'm so sorry,' I said to her.

'Don't worry about me,' she said, staring right at Roger. 'You watch out for yourself.'


Roger's jealousy got worse and worse over the weeks and it became clear that he didn't want me to see anyone or do anything. On another day I was on my way back from the corner shop when I met one of the neighbours opposite who had a new baby. She had the little girl swaddled in a pretty blanket.

'Oh congratulations,' I said. The baby looked so sweet.

Suddenly, Roger burst out of our front door with a bright red face. He marched straight across the road, grabbed me by the hair and hauled me back towards the house without saying so much as a word. I knew why. He had told me to fetch him something and, as far as he was concerned, stopping to talk to a neighbour was an unnecessary and rebellious delay. Behind me, the woman was horrified.

'Do you want me to call the police?' she called after me as I disappeared into the house.

'No,' I said, gritting my teeth against the pain in my scalp. 'No. It's fine.'

I was miserable but I wanted to deal with the problems myself. The idea of anyone else being involved mortified me. I had wanted my marriage to be perfect. I had believed it when Roger told me that he loved me. And now, as that image cracked and crumbled I felt that it was all my fault. Here I was, trapped again, with no money, no family and no friends. The echoes of my childhood were deafening.

'You're useless,' he ranted at me. 'Just look at you!'

And I believed him. I wanted to hide away, to withdraw from sight.

One of the neighbours tried to help. Old Mrs Burgess had probably seen just about everything in her day. One afternoon, when Roger was out, there was a rap on the door.

'Hello, pet,' she said kindly. 'Can I come in?'

I glanced up and down the street, nervously. Roger had gone over to Belle Vue and wouldn't be back until late. I nodded and let her into the hallway.

Everyone on the street knew what was going on. Roger made no secret of it. When I was growing up my father had made a big effort to cover his systematic violence and abuse. By contrast, Roger thought he had a perfect right to grab me by the hair or scream at me in public. In a small community like Compass Street I was painfully aware that all my neighbours knew what my husband was like.

Mrs Burgess sighed. She had kind blue eyes and a steady air that gave her dignity. 'I'm sorry for your trouble,' she said. 'Is there anything that I can do for you, love?'

I felt like crying but I held everything in. 'No. No. It's fine.'

'Are you sure?'

I cast my eyes to the floor. 'Yes.'

All my life having anyone else involved had only made things worse. I was determined to deal with this myself. I could bear anything as long as it was only up to me. I'd fix it. I'd survive. I always had. Mrs Burgess reached out and touched my arm.

'You know where I live,' she said. 'If you ever change your mind.'

Slowly, Roger got worse. Sometimes there were a couple of days when things seemed almost normal, but then, without any warning he flew into a jealous rage. He didn't trust me, or anything that I said.

'No wonder none of your family want you, you're disgusting' he screamed at me one night when he had been questioning me about my past. He refused to believe that I hadn't had any boyfriends before him.

'Just tell me. Just tell me,' he shouted over and over again.

'There wasn't anyone,' I swore.

It was desperate. I wasn't lying to him – there had never been anyone in the way that Roger meant and I was too afraid to tell him about the terrible things that had really happened. I wanted my past to remain where it was. I had been the one who had suffered it and dealt with it, and to air it for his dissection, his mocking condemnation and intolerant opinions, would have been too painful. I hid my bruises under long sleeves and kept away from the neighbours.

Over the weeks I felt worse and worse. My whole world contracted into the tiny rooms inside the house. I shied away from the door if anyone knocked and tried to stay out of sight of people passing my window and casually looking in. I didn't think I was of any value; I believed it when Roger screamed abuse at me and I took the beatings without fighting back.

Worse than the beatings were his violent, unwanted sexual attentions. In his bizarre fantasy life, he saw me as a slut and ordered me to do ever-more degrading things that made me feel sick to the stomach. It might start with him insisting I went out of the house without underwear on, then deteriorate into situations in which I was used like a piece of filth from the gutter. In all of the scenarios he wanted me to act out, he was totally dominant and if I ever baulked at anything, it would end with me being brutally beaten and raped by him.

What he didn't know was that my terror in those situations was absolutely real. Every time, I would relive the night I was raped in Johannesburg by a man who stank of beer and sweat, who grabbed my hair, yanked my head back and grunted, 'Shut up, you dirty slut!' I remembered the panicky feeling of not being able to breathe when he grabbed my throat, the punches and kicks, and that mean expression in his eyes. Roger did all this to me and more, night after night, but there was nothing I could do except put up with it. At that time there was no court in the land that would accept that a husband could 'rape' his own wife. It simply wasn't recognized.

\* \* \*

Then one day while I was washing, I noticed that my breasts were painful. I actually flinched as I rubbed them with the soap. Wrapping a towel around me, I caught a glimpse of myself in the tiny mirror over the sink. In that moment I counted the days and realized what had happened – and despite everything I was over the moon. I must have been about two months gone. Perhaps this would make everything better. Surely, surely.

'Roger,' I said that night when he got home. 'I'm feeling a bit strange. I think I'm going to have a baby.'

# Chapter Six

Roger was pleased about the baby, or at least I thought he was – he didn't say much. But for that matter, neither did I. I was quietly ecstatic. The pregnancy didn't stop him constantly demeaning me, of course, but now we had a secret together. In the first weeks we didn't tell a soul.

One Sunday we went to his parents' house for lunch. It was the usual overwhelming Lethbridge onslaught, though now we were married Roger openly criticized and mocked me in front of his family and sometimes they joined in.

'You look a state,' he picked on my appearance. 'Look at you in that old dress. What a sight!'

I was mortified. I had never cared much about clothes and I knew I didn't turn myself out smartly like Roger's pretty sisters. Of course, now that he controlled the budget I was never allowed any money to buy new clothes but I didn't mention that. Instead I hung my head and stayed completely silent.

Roger's mother had come to openly dislike me by this time. It was a particular bugbear for her that I didn't have any family.

'Judy must have done something really awful in the past,' Roger said, 'because she won't talk about it.'

Mrs Lethbridge eyed me up and down and I knew she was disappointed with her son's choice of wife. I wasn't what she'd hoped for. I dreaded going over there, even though it was the only time that I left Compass Street to do something that should have been sociable.

That Sunday I felt sick and I couldn't finish my meal.

'Is my food not good enough for you?' Mrs Lethbridge snapped.

I didn't want to tell her that I was suffering from morning sickness and Roger didn't step in to defend me, so I just shook my head silently and looked at my lap.

'See how useless you are,' Roger said on the way home on the bus. 'Can't take you anywhere. Keep your bloody eyes to the floor, I don't want you looking out.'

In his paranoia he had convinced himself that if I looked up, and my eyes caught a man inside or outside the bus, I was flirting with him. Often I was punished for that when we got home and protesting my innocence only made the screaming and the beating worse. He'd slap me, punch me or hit me with the poker or any other implement that came to hand, fuelled by a rage that I was a whore who was lying and cheating and couldn't be trusted. Looking back, I see now that his jealousy was pathological, almost verging on clinical insanity. That's the only explanation I can think of. But back then, I still didn't know how far from normal married life mine was.

Being pregnant changed things for me. It gave me a sense of purpose and I was excited about the future despite everything. I counted the months until I was due to give birth and planned my first trip to the doctor for when I was three or four months gone. Every day I felt the subtle changes in my body and I treasured those feelings, keeping them to myself. Each time I sensed something different I convinced myself that after the birth, things would surely change.

Much to Roger's amusement, I scrubbed the small bedroom upstairs. We might not have much, but at least it would be clean and tidy. Roger's granddad, who lived over the road, gave us several half tins of paint, rolls of odd wallpaper, and bits and pieces of D.I.Y. equipment so I set to painting and decorating the house. From the moment I knew that I was pregnant, it was very important that I did everything to be a wonderful mother. Back in South Africa, during the very worst times – when I was beaten senseless by Dad the night he recaptured me after my escape to the circus; or staring at my bloodied, puffed-up face in a station toilet mirror after being raped in a back alley – I got myself through by imagining how I would bring up my children if I was ever lucky enough to have any. I had so much love to give and I was just aching for someone to give it to.

Roger didn't change, though. He squirreled away every penny he earned, drank a great deal and gambled what was left on the slot machines. He did give me a housekeeping allowance but it was tiny and out of that I had to buy the expensive food that he liked – bacon and eggs and meat. I couldn't afford that kind of thing for myself as well, and as a consequence we ate different meals. For myself I made soup out of a few vegetables and a bone that the butcher would either give me or sell for a penny or two. A lot of the time I was hungry and during the pregnancy I found myself craving meat and other luxuries, but there was no way I could afford them.

One night, a few weeks into the pregnancy, I felt very tired. Roger had gone to the pub that evening with his uncle and I wasn't sure when he might be back. Roger's extended family was huge and many of them lived quite close by. It meant he was out of the house quite a bit in the evenings and that was fine by me.

I had to get some sleep, so I made some food and left it on the kitchen table for when he got in. Then I went upstairs and fell asleep immediately. I had been painting all day and the pregnancy was taking it out of me. I was exhausted.

A few hours later I woke up with a jolt. Roger was shaking me so hard that the bed was moving beneath me. I jerked into consciousness and immediately my heart pounded with terror. The room was completely dark and I couldn't see anything. Roger was shouting. His breath stank of beer and he was furious.

'What the bloody hell do you think you're doing?' he screamed. 'I come home, my dinner's cold and you're in bed, you lazy bitch.'

He hauled me out from under the covers as I tried to find my footing and then dragged me behind him across the wooden floor. My mind was racing – it was always better to just let Roger rage. Any resistance was futile and only made things worse. Still, it was dark and I was terrified. I knew that he was usually even more violent than normal when he'd been drinking.

'Christ,' he shouted. 'What the hell am I going to do with you?'

Still sleepy, I was completely disorientated as he pushed me ahead of him into the black hallway and gave me a shove in the direction of the stairs. In the dark I stumbled and lost my balance, falling awkwardly onto the stairs and tumbling for several feet until I hit the floor of the hallway below. It happened so quickly that I was confused and all the time Roger was screaming: 'You been out screwing other men? That's why you're tired, isn't it?'

As I landed, a sharp jab of pain in my stomach crippled me. It was difficult to breathe. I tried to get to my feet, but it hurt too much. Roger took the steps easily and, showing no concern for my welfare, grabbed me by the arm and hauled me into the kitchen. He pushed me roughly against the cooker. I felt another sharp jab in my stomach and tried to bend double. Roger caught me and pushed me upright, shouting right into my face.

'… Too much to expect my bleeding wife to cook a bleeding meal for me when I get home, is it?'

My breathing was shallow and I felt sick. I could feel things weren't right in my body and my mind was racing with the possibilities. Over-riding everything else was the thought that I had to protect the baby. And then, sickeningly, I felt something sticky between my legs. I looked down and in horror, saw that there was blood pouring out of me.

'The baby, Roger,' I gasped and he stopped in his tracks, seeing what had happened and realizing that this was serious.

'Stay there.'

Roger ran out of the house. In a panic, I pressed my legs together to try to stem the crimson flow that was leaking onto the floor. I thought if I just stayed still it wouldn't get any worse. My mind was racing. I was scared that Roger might just disappear and then what would I do, standing bleeding in my own kitchen, waiting for help that wasn't on its way? That wasn't his tactic though. A few minutes later he came back through the door, his face flushed. We didn't have a phone in the house so he had run all the way to the call box on the main road.

'I dialled 999,' he said. 'They're sending an ambulance.'

A tear rolled down my cheek and a sense of relief flooded me. He does care after all, I thought to myself.

The ambulance came quickly. Two paramedics put me on a stretcher, carried me into the street and loaded me into the back of the vehicle.

'How far gone are you, love?' one of them asked.

'About three months I think, maybe a little more' I said.

I couldn't bear to ask about the baby. I was too afraid of what the paramedic might say. Roger didn't come in the ambulance. He was the last person I wanted near me in any case. One of the men sat beside the stretcher for the journey to Crumpsall Hospital. He was encouraging and kind, but I found it difficult to speak. I was so worried. The only thing that mattered was the baby being all right.

'We've radioed ahead,' he said. 'The doctor will be waiting.'

At the hospital they rushed me up to the ward. The doctor examined me quickly and gave the nurse instructions I didn't understand. The bleeding hadn't stopped and I had cramps in my stomach that knocked the wind out of me. I didn't mind the pain, as long as everything was going to be all right. A nurse smiled apologetically and held my hand. I could tell from the look in her eyes that something was very wrong.

'Oh no,' I thought, as a sense of annihilation engulfed me.

The doctor simply said 'I'm sorry.'

It felt as though my world was caving in. The only good thing in my life was gone, finished. I couldn't take it in completely. I just lay there in black despair.

'We need to do a D and C,' the doctor said, and then, seeing that I had no idea what he was talking about, he explained, 'We need to go inside you and take out anything that is still in there.'

I felt wracked with grief but I was so shocked that I didn't even cry when they wheeled me into the theatre.

Afterwards I was tucked into a bed on a ward with eight other women. It was late and I was completely devastated. My baby was gone. The nurses had been kind but for them it was a routine occurrence. I felt totally stripped, as if everything Roger had ever said about me being useless was all true. The nurse had left a cup of tea and a biscuit beside the bed, but I couldn't touch them. I stared blankly at the empty hallway outside the ward and pulled the covers right up to my eyes. I had failed and all I wanted now was to hide from the world.

It must have been about midnight when I saw Roger striding up the corridor. For a moment I felt a sense of relief. Here was my husband coming to visit me. Surely he was as devastated as I was? Then, as he got closer, I realized he was still drunk. I glanced round. The other women on the ward had also lost their babies. They were mostly asleep, apart from one who was sitting up reading in the corner. I saw her glance towards the door as Roger came through. He didn't even say hello to me.

'You are bloody useless, aren't you?' he started in a whisper, and I thought at least his voice was low. However, as he proceeded into his tantrum, the volume increased.

'Well, I don't care,' he hammered home. 'It wasn't my baby, anyway. Christ knows what you get up to all day, you two-faced bitch. It could have been anyone's!'

His face was livid and contorted with anger and his eyes were bloodshot. I knew that everyone on the ward was able to hear those last words. The volume was getting too loud for anyone to sleep through.

'I'm glad the baby's gone,' he said, grabbing hold of my arm. 'Little bastard.'

Then he turned and, losing it completely, he began to verbally abuse all the other women, who were waking up sleepily and staring in disbelief.

'You're all whores,' he screamed. 'All of you! Sluts and bitches!' he howled.

From the silent hallway I could see a flutter of nurses and a security guard approaching Roger, who was so loud by now that they had probably heard everything he'd said from several wards away. Everyone was awake and sitting up. I didn't say a word. I couldn't. I wanted to disappear.

Roger continued regardless. 'You women! Bloody cows! Two-faced slags!'

'Excuse me, sir,' said a low, male voice and the security guard put his hand on Roger's shoulder.

Roger shrugged him off and continued to shout in an uncontrolled fashion in my general direction. 'You think I don't know anything, you bloody tart. Well I do. I'm onto you.'

'That's enough, sir,' the security guard said quietly but firmly.

Roger still didn't stop. He continued to hurl abuse as the guard pulled him away. I watched, horrified, as my husband was escorted down the corridor, his shrieks receding. I could feel everyone in the room pitying me.

'You all right, love?' the woman in the next bed asked gently.

I nodded and sank back down onto the pillows.

'What a bastard,' I heard one of the other women say.

Then a nurse drew the curtains around my bed.

'He's just upset,' I tried to excuse him as the tears came and my chest heaved.

'Now, now,' she said kindly and gave me a hug. 'You didn't need that as well, did you?'

Two days later I was discharged and I went home to Compass Street. Roger was waiting. As I came through the door he broke down.

'I'm so sorry,' he said simply, crying. 'Here.' He handed me a present.

It was a pretty, wooden, music box. I opened the lid. It sounded like a piano. I think it was playing Auld Lang Syne. Roger looked really devastated by what he'd done and I was glad to think he finally realized that he couldn't behave that way any more. We left the music playing and we cried together.

'We'll try for another baby,' he promised. 'I'm sorry, Judy. I'll never do anything like that again.'

I wanted to believe him. After all, he was my husband. I set a lot of store by the fact Roger had apologized but I was still afraid of him. Fear was a familiar emotion for me, though, and I coped with it well. I actually felt optimistic. In contrast, my father had never once taken responsibility for his violent actions or said sorry. Sitting now, crying next to me, it appeared that Roger was distraught at what he'd done. I hoped that told its own story. Maybe this had needed to happen to make everything change. Maybe things would be alright now.

# Chapter Seven

Within a few months I fell pregnant again. I was excited but also scared in case anything went wrong. At nine weeks I bled again and while I lay on the floor, filled with despair, Roger called an ambulance once more. This time I kept the pregnancy though I was told to stay in bed and rest as much as possible. As I lay under the sheets, I willed that baby to be fine with every fibre in my entire being. Thankfully, the bleeding stopped and the doctor gave me instructions to take better care of myself. Under these orders Roger's regime slackened a little and although I still had to account for the housekeeping money, make meals to his instructions and prepare his clothes for him, I noticed that he flew off the handle considerably less frequently.

Still, I was deeply unhappy. I desperately wanted to share my whole soul with my husband but however hard I tried he simply didn't accept me. And though the beatings were less frequent, nothing I did was ever good enough. Roger constantly changed the goal posts so I never knew quite what he wanted and over the months his jealousy and possessiveness remained as powerful as ever.

He repeatedly demanded to know all about my life before I arrived at Belle Vue. Anyone else would have seen how much it upset me to think about my past and left well alone, but Roger was a natural bully and in that house he had absolute power.

'You're hiding something seedy, aren't you? Something sordid, you filthy bitch,' he persisted. 'You can't have grown up without a family. Why did they chuck you out then? What did you do?'

I couldn't answer – I just wasn't capable of talking about it, and I'm sure he wouldn't have believed me anyway. My refusal to tell him about my past often led to yet another tirade about the evils of women. But how could I begin to tell him? How could I explain that my father was a monster, that he'd torn me away from my mother and sisters, that I'd endured years of violence and abuse? Roger would never understand what that felt like. He'd only ever use it as ammunition against me. At least, I thought to myself, if I can just show him I am not like all these women in his head, he'll stop.

So I stuck with it. I thought it was the right thing to do. I was not one to give up just because the going was rough. I had been severely conditioned all my life to be subservient and made to feel that everyone else was right. As Roger shouted at me, I could have been right back in Johannesburg with my father playing his sadistic power games, or even further back to the day when Freda beat me with a curtain rod after my shoe fell down a grating. I had no real sense of myself, but I was tough and determined to keep trying. Once we had a baby, maybe he would calm down. Surely he would?

\* \* \*

The labour, when the time came, was harsh, but pain never bothered me – I was inured to it. I was only afraid that something would go wrong for the baby. In the end, my beautiful daughter was a forceps delivery. I held her in my arms and enjoyed the proudest and happiest feelings of my whole life. In that moment it was impossible to understand how my own mother could ever have given me up. The love I felt for my baby burned deep inside me. I would have done anything for this tiny bundle. If she had been snatched away, I would have followed her to the ends of the earth, fighting tooth and nail to keep her.

With this child in my arms, I remembered my own mother's coldness. I thought about the day when I was ten and I had come to visit her, after years of no contact, and she didn't give me a proper hug or ask how I was. It was as if even as she faced me, my mother had her back turned. I had never been wanted.

'What will we call her?' Roger asked, calling me back to the moment and my own, precious baby.

I stared at the tiny bundle in my arms and felt the enchantment of her lovely, blue eyes. 'Helen?' I suggested.

He nodded. 'All right.'

Even in that matter, though, Roger wanted to let me know that he was the boss and later, when he went to register the birth, he gave the baby the name Judith Helen. In his family it was traditional to give a baby a family name, but it hurt that he hadn't discussed it with me. It was hardly the worst thing that Roger had ever done but still, it demonstrated his need to have complete control of everything.

'Little Judith Helen,' I tried it out.

Just before my fifth birthday, I'd been sent to live in an orphanage for a couple of years and the nuns there believed in a harsh regime that would train us to be obedient. One nun in particular, Sister Bridget, had been very cruel to me and I remembered how she almost spat the 'th' sound at the end of my name. Every time I said the word 'Judith', it brought back that horrible memory of her voice and the way she used to hit me with her cane for tiny infractions like putting a spoon in the kitchen drawer the wrong way round. I didn't want my daughter's name to bring such nasty associations into my head, so I soon started calling her Jude.

Back in Compass Street when I got home from the hospital, I hit my stride straightaway. When Jude smiled my heart melted. Somehow motherhood came naturally to me; it was almost feral. Instinctively I just wanted to gather her up in my arms and hold her close to me all day long. I loved looking after her and spent my days organizing feeds, bathing her, changing her, talking to her and taking her out for fresh air in the park. Roger only gave me permission to take the baby as far as the clinic but I would stretch the route to include a walk in the sunshine whenever I could. He was out a lot – sometimes I'd see him in the distance, playing the slot machines in the local café. Money was very tight. I know he earned a decent salary from his daredevil rides in the Globe but he didn't increase the housekeeping money he gave me even when there was a baby in the house and in those days there was no child benefit from the government until you had your second child.

Roger's tirades about my incompetence continued in one long stream from the moment he opened the front door until the moment he left the house again. It was clear that he was disappointed that Jude was a girl. 'Just some moronic shell,' was how he described any female. I wanted to protect my baby from this and I tried even harder to keep out of Roger's way and have everything set out the way he liked it.

'Oh you're too good to be true, you are! I mean is this baby even mine?' he'd shout in a temper.

Sometimes I really feared what he might do to her. I could take anything for myself, but I was worried sick that he'd lose it one day and not realize how small and vulnerable Jude was.

When I got pregnant again quickly I was delighted on the one hand, but very worried about how Roger might react. After all, he was so determined that I was sleeping with every man in the district that to him another pregnancy was just an opportunity to let accusations fly. If the baby was another girl I knew that he'd be even more upset. These fears were well and truly brought home when I did eventually tell him.

'This baby isn't mine,' he raged. 'I'll bet you've been with every man you've ever spoken to, you slut.'

It went on for hours and nothing I could say or do calmed him down.

I had no idea at this stage how I could ever change my situation but I willed myself to believe that if I could just keep going somehow I would find a way out as soon as it was possible. I was beginning to accept that I didn't have the power to change Roger but I was completely isolated, with no family to turn to and no friends to talk to. I had no money and nowhere to go. It felt as though I was well and truly caught in a trap.

\* \* \*

Having a toddler, it was difficult to take enough rest during that second pregnancy but Jude was a good kid and somehow I made it work. Over the months, as my bump grew larger, I planned for the birth. I was very grateful when Roger's mother offered to look after Jude when the time came for me to go into hospital. Roger had never looked after our daughter on his own and I was afraid of leaving her in his care but Mrs Lethbridge, on the other hand, knew how to look after babies, having had ten of her own. However much she disliked me, she would never take it out on her fourteen-month-old granddaughter.

The second time I went into labour very late – it was three weeks after my due date according to the doctor. In the end, I suffered a thrombosis and they decided to induce the birth. Under the circumstances it was no surprise that it was touch and go throughout the whole labour. After several hours the baby was born, but he was blue from a deficiency of oxygen in his blood.

'It's a boy,' the nurse smiled, 'but we need to put him into the special care unit for now.'

I felt a huge rush of love swiftly followed by a wave of concern. My second baby was here, and the fact he was a boy would please Roger no end. But would he be all right?

The nurses didn't even want to let me see him because they thought his colour would distress me, and he was taken away immediately while the team turned their attention to patching me up. I was exhausted.

'You need some sleep, love,' the sister said, but all I could think about was my baby.

'Will he be OK?' I asked anyone who would listen.

'With God's help,' the sister told me.

That didn't reassure me at all.

In the end both the baby and I stayed in hospital for a week or so. He was given excellent care but for years afterwards the tip of one of his ears remained blue and from that very first day he had difficulty breathing. The nurses showed me how to prepare a steam inhaler and gave me instructions for his care. It was a lot to take on. I was still only twenty-one myself and struggling to keep my head above water in a grim marriage, but I listened carefully and made sure I understood everything I had to do.

Roger arrived well after all the action was over. As expected, as soon as he heard the baby was a boy he was pleased as punch. 'He's got my eyes,' he said proudly. 'So, what name will we give my little man?'

We decided on David. 'How about David John?' I said, remembering what had happened with Jude's registration.

'Fine,' he said. 'David John it is,' but then he registered the baby with his own name as a middle name anyway.

The months that followed were particularly difficult. Despite his pride at having produced a male heir, I was bewildered by Roger's apparent lack of care for his children. I would have laid down my life in a heartbeat for either of them. In contrast, Roger simply wasn't interested. He thought looking after the children was woman's work and wouldn't even push a pram.

'I'm no sissy,' he said.

David was a needy baby – his bronchial difficulties took a lot of my time and I was very worried that Jude wasn't getting enough attention. I felt hurt on her behalf when I was busy giving David medical care and her father wasn't on hand. It wouldn't have taken much for him to sit and tell her a story or give her a cuddle on his knee. In fact, I think Roger resented the fact that my attention was focused elsewhere and I wasn't merely his slave any more. If anything, his temper tantrums and violent outbursts were increasing around that time.

In November 1966, a few weeks after David was born, things reached crisis point. Roger lost his temper, and this time it was with the children. They were typical babies – noisy and needy – and he became angry and frustrated and began to physically discipline them. One day Jude crawled towards the fire and I pulled her back.

'No silly. Hot. It's hot,' I gently chastised her.

'You have to show her!' Roger snapped and, grabbing her, he pressed her little hand onto the grille in front of the flames. She screamed at the top of her voice with pain and acute terror. Nothing like that had ever happened in her young life and she had no way of understanding it. As I rushed to run her wound under cold water and try to calm her down, Roger looked on mockingly and I felt hatred towards him for the first time. How could anyone do that to a child?

I had a sudden flashback to the day my father tied me to a kitchen chair and forced me to eat spoonfuls of soot from the fireplace. I was choking, my eyes streaming, my chest heaving for breath, utterly and completely petrified. It was that incident, when I was four years old, that led to me being hospitalized and then taken into an institution for the next three years. I couldn't help but see the parallels between Roger's and my father's behaviour and I was completely devastated.

Jude cried for over an hour, and that night something in me hardened. He could hit me all he liked but I couldn't stand by and watch him injure my children. I couldn't risk them being taken away from me if social services thought I wasn't protecting them properly. I couldn't risk them being hurt any more. The very next day I took my life in my hands and contacted the police. If Roger had found out where I had gone, the beating would have been merciless, but I had to do something. I didn't want my children to suffer the kind of bullying that I had endured from my father and that was that.

I wheeled the pram to Openshawe police station on Ashton Old Road and furtively darted inside. There were no female officers but I was put in a room and told to talk to the sergeant on duty, a huge man who hardly seemed to be listening to me, even when I showed him Jude's blistered fingers.

'Look, love,' he said, once I had blurted my story out, 'this is a domestic situation.'

'But please,' I begged, 'I'm afraid of what he might do.'

The officer wasn't sympathetic. 'He pays the rent does he, your husband?'

'Yes.'

'Well he's master of the house then.'

'He said if I left, he'd kill me.'

The policeman shrugged his shoulders. 'He wants you to stay,' he said, as if it was only a natural reaction.

And that was it. I left the station devastated.

The following day I tried again to get help. I wheeled the pram to Ashton social services department and repeated my story.

'You could go to a shelter,' the lady said, 'but there's a good chance your children might be taken into care.'

I looked at Jude and David in the pram and realized that wasn't even an option. I wouldn't be able to bear it. I could never desert them.

'OK,' I said. 'Thanks.'

And I left.

I didn't know where to turn next. After another sleepless night I realized that I had to find someone to talk to. That alone would be a big help and in desperation I took a big step. I phoned my mother.

I hadn't seen my mother since I got back from South Africa five years earlier. I'd stayed with her and my sisters for two long weeks, trying desperately to fit into a family I hadn't been part of since I was three years old. But the stay descended into bitterness and suspicion on her part, as she and my sisters accused me of 'stealing their things' and tried to hide me away from the neighbours like a guilty little secret. I'd left to start work at Speedy's and hadn't seen her since so she'd never even met her grandchildren. I sent her a note after each birth, but she hadn't shown any more interest in Jude or David than she had in me when I was growing up. Nonetheless I hoped that maybe she might be able to help me now. After all, we were both mothers. Jude and David were her grandchildren. Surely she would want to be involved?

'Hello, it's Judy,' I started, awkwardly.

'Oh yes,' Mum said coldly. It was not the response I'd hoped for, but at least she didn't hang up. Grudgingly, she arranged to meet me in Manchester.

I put the kids in the pram and headed for the city centre, a couple of miles away. I was running over things in my mind. If anything happened to the children I would never forgive myself. Perhaps this was Mum's chance to help me. If she could lend a sympathetic ear maybe I would find a way out of my disastrous marriage. She had got away from my Dad, after all. Surely there was some advice she could offer?

It was already dark and it had been a cold day. I blew on Jude's fingers to keep them warm and bundled them both up tightly in a blanket.

'We're going out now. Keep that blanket round you,' I said as I wheeled them along.

We met outside a restaurant in the centre of town. Mum was with my stepfather, Paddy, who had driven her into the city. She gave me a half-hearted hello.

'So these are the children,' she said.

I could tell straightaway that she viewed this meeting purely as a hassle. She wasn't glad to see us. She barely glanced at Jude and David, who were staring with wide-eyed curiosity. There was an awkward pause.

'I just really need to talk to you, Mum …' I started, but my voice trailed off.

She looked at me with a perplexed expression. I could see her wondering what on earth I wanted from her. 'Maybe you'd better come home with us,' she said. 'We've got a car.'

The journey was silent. Back at the house, my youngest half-sister Lily was in the living room.

'Shall I take these kids upstairs?' she asked.

Jude and David were tired because it was getting late and I was very grateful that they would be taken out of hearing. Mum went into the kitchen to make some tea and I followed her. I felt like a stranger in this house but I needed her to listen to me and this seemed like my best chance.

It was not to be. Before I had a chance even to say a word, I heard a commotion at the front door. There was hammering and then raised, shouting voices. My blood froze as I realized that it was Roger. I've got no idea how he found me but I can only think that he either followed me that day, or he had found Mum's address on one of my letters and when he discovered I was missing he came straight round there.

'Where is she? Where is she?' Roger was yelling.

Mum continued to put on the kettle and completely ignored what was going on.

'I've done it now,' I thought, and my whole body shook as Roger launched himself into the kitchen in a fury. He didn't say a word to Mum, just pushed me up against the sink threateningly while screaming abuse and shaking me hard. I looked towards her for some kind of protection but, to my horror, she avoided my eyes and deliberately turned her back on me. I was on my own.

When Roger finally stopped shaking me, Paddy came into the kitchen.

'She's a nightmare! You don't know what she's like,' Roger told him.

Paddy shrugged. 'I don't want anything to do with this. Here,' he reached into his pocket and brought out a £5 note. 'Take this and get her out of here,' he said to Roger. 'And I don't want either of you to come to my house again.'

My heart sank. Here I was, betrayed and abandoned again. Slowly I went upstairs, rubbing my arm where he had gripped me. I picked up my children. Why did nobody care? Why could they not just have listened? I hadn't wanted much from them. As we left the house Roger shouted for everyone to hear, 'Just wait till I get you home.'

The last thing I saw was my mother shutting the door behind me. She wouldn't meet my eyes.

Back at Compass Street a wave of nausea hit me. It didn't feel like my own home any more. It was difficult to accept that my mother had abandoned me yet again. Worse still was the fact that she had let down her own grandchildren. I had no money and nowhere to go. I was terrified of what Roger would do. I'd tried everything I could think of.

After I had put the kids to bed, I crept downstairs. Roger was working on his bike in the back room. He cast a glance at me through the open door. There was a smug expression on his face. He had, after all, come through the whole thing £5 richer and the undisputed winner. The look in his eyes said, 'You belong to me. There's nothing you can do.'

It was the first time he had met my mother but he showed no interest in her at all. He just said, 'None of your shit family wants you, not even your own mother. You must have done something really bad for them to throw you out.'

From that day on, I began to live in the kitchen. I felt utterly hopeless, and in the depths of my depression I shrank inside myself. I closed the living room curtains, too afraid to be seen by neighbours. I didn't answer the door to the window cleaner, milkman or postman. There was no point. No one cared. No one was going to help. The kitchen was tiny and there was hardly enough room for the two children to crawl around. I could open the back door, but bad weather often kept us inside. There was no radio or TV and I spent the day keeping busy as best I could until Roger came home and started his tirade yet again.

That winter, in the cold and the damp, David's bronchitis got worse and the doctor suggested that a warmer climate would make a big difference to the baby. Then, around Easter 1967 Roger came home with the news that Speedy had sold the Globe to a Russian impresario called Charley Henchis. Mr Henchis was taking the act abroad to Beirut as part of the after-dinner entertainment in a casino. I didn't know where Beirut was exactly, but I guessed it would be warm. When Roger was offered a job riding in the new show he snapped it up. The move would mean a big pay rise.

'What do you say, Judy?' he asked. 'It'll be a new start.'

I thought of my little boy, straining for every breath. Perhaps this was a godsend. Any change had to be a good thing.

'Yeah. Let's go,' I said.

# Chapter Eight

M r Henchis was planning to open the show in Beirut the following year, but the act as it stood wasn't quite right for him.

'What I really want,' he said, 'is something that's even more of a draw. Two men riding motorbikes, well,' he shrugged to indicate that this simply wasn't enough. 'But,' he continued, 'if one of the riders was female, now that would be something. I wondered, Mr Lethbridge, if you would consider training your wife to ride in the Globe?'

I was shocked and excited by this but, like Mr Henchis, I knew the decision wasn't up to me. I didn't say a word and waited for Roger to reply.

'Yes,' he said slowly, obviously examining the proposition from all angles. 'Why not?'

The two men shook hands on it. Both Roger and I would be earning far more than we could in the UK, though Roger, of course, insisted that his pay packet would be bigger than mine.

'She'll be the second rider,' he insisted. 'After all, I have all the experience.'

Mr Henchis agreed on £30 a week for Roger and £28 for me. It was a fortune in 1967, but I wasn't thinking about the money or even the prospect of working again. I was simply keen for little David to be somewhere the weather would be good for his chest.

'Right then,' said Roger. 'We better sort this out.'

Vicky, my old colleague in the Australian Air Aces, lived in a farmhouse just outside the town and there was some land attached to it; she agreed that we could set up a practice globe there. It would take months for me to learn to ride since I was starting from scratch. I had never as much as switched on the engine of a motorbike before.

For convenience' sake, and no doubt to save money, Roger arranged for us to give up our lease on Compass Street and move into an old mill that was at the end of Vicky's field.

'It'll be easier,' he said. 'Everything will be together and we can practise as much as we like.'

I had a vision of a pretty, English mill-house. The truth was much less appealing.


As we drove up to the field and I saw the place for the first time my heart sank. The mill was nothing but a burnt-out shell. The whole of one wall had fallen into the stream so the house was open to the elements on one side. It was impossible to live on the ground floor, which was partly flooded. The first floor was in a better condition with two rooms but the back room was filled with old motorbikes and this left just one room intact. The only way to get in was by climbing a 20-foot ladder running up the side of the building. For a street kid, a place like this would have been a haven but I couldn't believe that any man would bring his wife and children there by choice.

I made my way up the ladder gingerly, holding David in my arms. He was only seven months old. I carefully stepped off onto the bare floorboards. The room was a state. The windows had no glass and the side of the building that was missing gave out onto a perilous drop. Huge water rats scuttled in and out of the water below. Compass Street had never been a palace, but the prospect of Jude and David living here horrified me. Jude was twenty-one months old and an active toddler.

'This'll be fine, Judy,' Roger said. 'You can do it up a bit.'

Ever the obedient wife, I flung myself into that straightaway. I found some plastic sheeting to cover the empty windows in the only room that had four walls. It took ages to nail everything into place but once it was done, this, at least, made it safe for Jude to toddle about. I bought some paint and freshened up the walls, which made the place seem lighter. We still had to get in and out using the ladder, which was no mean feat with two small children.

'Just come over and use the toilet in the farmhouse any time you like,' Vicky offered. It meant a few minutes' walk across the field, but at least there was clean running water and a toilet there. The children were both still in nappies, thank goodness, but there was nowhere proper to wash them in the mill house. It felt as if there were pans of water constantly boiling, whether to soak endless nappies in Napisan, prepare David's inhaler, or simply keep the kids clean.

We lived in the mill house for almost a year. Roger's temper continued to erupt regularly and he often laid into me. One evening I heard him coming across the field, already shouting abuse, though I couldn't make out what he was saying. As he climbed the ladder it became clearer.

'Damn tick. I go into the shop and you've put something on bloody tick. What do you do with all the money I give you, Judy?'

I froze. I had run out of cash that day and asked the local shopkeeper if I could take a tin of corned beef and pay her the following week when my child allowance came through. Somehow Roger had found out. I looked round desperately. The little ones were playing on the floor. I didn't know what to do.

Then before I knew it, Roger had launched himself into the room from the top of the ladder. He grabbed me by the throat and tried to throw me through the huge window. The space was covered by plastic sheeting but it could easily have snapped off the nails, leaving me hurtling twenty feet into the river below.

'He just wants to get rid of me,' I panicked.

I struggled out of his grip but there was nowhere to run. If I went into the three-walled area I would have been thrown out for sure. Roger was so livid that he picked up the children's baby walker and threw it at my head. I dodged it and it tore smack through the plastic sheet, leaving the room with a perilous drop wide open on that side. I knew I had to find some help this time – Roger was out to kill me – but Vicky's place was way across the field and I had the kids to consider. Then I remembered that Pepe and Kiki, the poodle trainers from Belle Vue, were staying in a caravan on the grounds not far from the mill.

'Right,' I thought. 'I'll have to run there.'

I made it to the ladder and Roger scrambled after me in a blind rage leaving the children alone in the room. I had to be as fast as I could. I was terrified to leave Jude and David alone with all the dangers in that mill-house, but even more scared of what would happen if I didn't get help. 'It's the lesser of two evils,' I thought. I ran until it felt as though my lungs would burst, and hammered on the caravan door.

Quickly I managed to blurt it all out to Pepe.

'Come on!' I begged. 'Please help me!'

Pepe had difficulty walking and needed a stick, but he followed me and was able to fend off Roger's rage enough to let me back into the house to protect the children.

It shocked Roger that Pepe stood up for me and he disappeared over the field, shouting to all and sundry about what a slut I was. Heaven knows where he went but he didn't come home for two days afterwards.

Life at the mill was difficult enough even without Roger's violent rages. The rats soon realized we had food stowed away and I would find their teeth marks embedded perfectly in the block of butter. They were intelligent creatures and chewed carefully through the packaging of the bread, stealing the loaf slice by slice once they had penetrated the greaseproof paper. It was pretty grim.

One time late at night I heard them in the kitchen area. I was in my pyjamas but I decided to try and see them off. I needed a weapon but the only things I could lay my hands on were a table knife and a big envelope. I ventured over, shaking the envelope to try to startle the intruders while brandishing the knife in my other hand.

'Get lost!' I shooed.

The kitchen area was right next to the missing wall and in the dark I had to be careful of the long drop into the river. As I approached, a huge rat the size of a cat launched itself towards me. I screamed.

'Oh my God!'

I hadn't realized quite how big they were. In panic, I flung my weapons to the ground, ran into the other room and slammed the door. The rat could have the stupid bread, I didn't care.

As they became more confident over the months we lived there, I was terrified that the rats might get into the other room and attack the children in their cots to get their bottles of milk. A couple of times in desperation I threw a knife again, to chase them off. I was constantly on my guard.

'Get out of here! Go on!' I shouted frantically, wishing I had Speedy's aim.


The mill-house might have been a disaster, but I enjoyed learning to ride in the Globe. I set up a baby swing on the frame that David could kick about in and put Jude in her buggy while I practised. First of all, I had to get used to kickstarting the bike and riding around. I had good balance so that wasn't too difficult. We set up an obstacle course to improve my steering and control. I had to ride round an old bale of hay and then in between some stones. Roger stood at the end of the field and shouted instructions. He was a terrible teacher. The truth was he didn't really want me to ride. He knew it would make me the star of the show instead of him and he resented that, but on the other hand, he'd agreed with Mr Henchis to teach me and knew that my progress reflected his ability. This meant that he was torn and pushed me constantly to do better while boosting his own ego by telling me how useless I was.

'Come on, Judy. You can do better than that, can't you? You're bloody hopeless!'

At first it was difficult even to stay upright and control my speed, but slowly I improved.

After a couple of weeks working on my basic riding skills, Roger started me in the Globe. He stood at the bottom of the cage and held the back seat of the bike then I had to ride round slowly. It was difficult. Roger was an assured rider who knew exactly what he was doing but I was a novice and the Globe was a confined space so any mistake became magnified. He sometimes shouted instructions and sometimes he didn't – my hearing was so bad anyway, that often I didn't catch what he was saying above the roar of the engine. At first I just drove round and round the base but I had difficulty controlling the speed and once I skidded out of control.

'Get out the way!' I screamed but Roger didn't move in time and I accidentally mowed him down.

'Jesus, Judy!' he complained, rubbing his leg. 'You trying to kill me or something, you stupid cow? You can't do anything right!'

Roger pushed me all the time while I was learning so I never mastered one skill before he insisted that I move to the next. Well before I was ready he rode his bike up one side of the cage and yelled at me to follow.

'I'm only just getting the hang of it,' I said.

'Come on,' he shouted impatiently. 'Give it a proper try.'

I knew I had to apply myself. With Roger pushing me so hard, accidents were inevitable. I spent hours riding a practice motorbike that stood on a frame of chain-driven rollers. One day the bike moved slightly and as it slipped off I fell across the chain and ripped my leg open. Unsurprisingly, Roger couldn't care less. This didn't stop the training even though I had to have stitches in my leg and for a while it was difficult to kickstart my engine. At close proximity and high speed it was a perilous business.

'It's just something you have to go through,' Roger said as I limped up the ladder and into the mill-house.

Meantime, Roger's brother Peter, who was now sixteen, had stuck to his guns about wanting a job in the amusement park. A few weeks into my training, Mr Henchis arranged for him to join us so that there would be a stand-in in Beirut whenever one was needed.

'Hi Judy!' he grinned as he strode across the field. I was doing circuits.

'She's bloody useless!' Roger immediately told him. 'Stand well back, for Christ's sake.'

Peter stared wistfully at the circuit. 'Can I have a shot?' he asked.

Roger loved being in charge and he agreed to train us together.

For me, it was great having Peter around and the kids adored him. Whenever he took a break he would get down on the floor to play with them in his good-natured, sunny fashion, and I loved to watch them. Peter and I worked well together. He was a natural rider and learned all the stunts very quickly. Roger tended to leave us alone to work out our own patterns. I think he was glad to be able to go off to the pub.

One day, during a taxing rehearsal we were trying to perfect a very difficult stunt – a three-minute act where one person rides around the centre at a set speed, and the other rides round the lower half of the Globe at a slower speed that keeps them level with the other bike. Anything to do with the Globe involves split-second timing. You have to be aware of exactly where the other bike is at all times because if you touch each other there will be a crash, and at high speed and in close quarters that means an explosion.

We were doing well. We'd been in there for well over an hour when we decided to have one last go. We'd just begun the dangerous bit when Peter's bike suddenly broke in half and he was flung to the bottom of the Globe with his mangled bike landing on top of him. I struggled to avoid the debris and bring my own bike to a halt. I was steering on instinct and finally toppled off and ended up in a pile at the bottom of the Globe on top of everything else.

Roger was away and there was no one nearby. I hauled myself to my feet and a searing pain shot up my leg. Gritting my teeth I began to search frantically among the wreckage to switch off the petrol taps. I knew that this was vital or Peter and I would both be torched to a crisp. I found the one on my bike, but Peter's was a mangled wreck and that took longer.

'Peter!' I shouted, trying to haul him out. 'Come on Peter.'

And then I gasped as I saw his face. It was a mess – there was blood everywhere. His nose and jaw had been smashed. I slowly helped him up.

'You alright?' Peter slurred, though it was difficult for him to speak.

'Yes, but we've got to get out of here.' One of the bikes had got jammed across the exit and the Globe would have to be opened from the outside.

I started shouting. Vicky was over in the farmhouse but that was a long way for my voice to carry. 'Help!' I howled, terrified. A lot of petrol had escaped before I could stem the flow and I knew there was still a chance it would ignite.

'Help!'

After what seemed like ages, the guy who lived in the basement flat at Vicky's house came by.

'Please open the cage,' I begged. 'Please. Quickly.'

The man pulled open the door.

'Oh hell,' he said when he caught sight of Peter as we both crawled out.

'I'm going to the house to get help,' I said and dragged myself across the field, my leg in agony.

Peter was in hospital for weeks having his jaw rewired, his nose set and his cuts stitched up. My leg was very badly bruised but I was riding again the next day.

'Just a dodgy bike,' Roger pronounced. 'The headstock must have gone.' And there was no let up in the training routine.

After several months I was ready and Peter was back on form. He had scars on his face but it didn't stop him smiling.

'Hey, Judy! That's brilliant!' he called from the sidelines the first time I managed to loop the loop on my own. I was the first woman ever to master this in the Globe.

'Not bad,' Roger nodded, and from him that was high praise.

Then, a few weeks before we were due to leave for Beirut I had a horrible shock. The family who lived in the house next door to Vicky's had become concerned about our living conditions and contacted the child welfare agency. The woman had seen me climbing precariously up the ladder. I could only take up one child at a time so I usually left Jude in the pram down in the field and took David up the ladder and then, when I had settled him in his cot, I went back and carried up Jude. The pram stayed in the field in all weathers and was often wet. I used to have to tip out the water before we used it.

'Bloody busybodies!' Roger snarled when we got a letter from the local welfare office saying they were sending social workers to inspect the mill-house.

I could hardly sleep. That summer I'd seen *Cathy Come Home* in the cinema. It had made a big impression on me not just because of the story but because it was one of the few times Roger took me out after we were married. The parents in the film, Cathy and Reg, had become homeless after Reg lost his job, and they had to live in a succession of illegal squats and shelters until finally social services took their two children into care because they were living in such bad conditions. It was a real tearjerker and the story cut very close to the bone for me. I thought that if anyone ever took my children away from me I would die. I rushed around making sure that everything in the mill-house was squeaky clean, fussing over every tiny detail.

'What if they take Jude and David?' I asked Roger, my voice choked with tears.

'They won't,' he growled. 'Bloody load of nonsense!'

Still, on the morning of the visit, Roger disappeared and left me to it. He had a real dread of authority figures. I was on my own.

The two men and a woman were wearing suits. As they climbed the 20-foot ladder I prayed that there wouldn't be any rats scampering about during their visit. Perhaps the large number of people in the room would make them wary of coming out. I willed the social workers to let us pass the inspection.

'Well, love, it's clean and tidy,' the lady said kindly as she looked around.

They asked how long we had been there and about our water supply. Vicky had said it was fine to show them the toilet we used up at the house, but they said they didn't have to inspect that. The woman smiled at Jude and David who were playing happily with some toys on the floor.

'We have a job in Beirut to go to,' I said. 'We'll be leaving soon.'

'How soon?'

'A month or two.'

It was still summertime. The mill would be warm enough until the weather turned in October. We had survived one winter there already but I could see why they were asking the question. The walls were damp as it was and if it was rainy or icy the ladder became treacherous. I was glad that we wouldn't have to face another winter there.

'It will be warm in Beirut,' I said, 'and it will help David's weak chest.'

'As long as you're gone in a few weeks, that's fine,' the man said decisively.

My face must have shown my relief.

'Don't worry, love,' he said, smiling. 'We can see you're a good Mum. You really care for these children. Just make sure you have enough ventilation for that calor gas, eh? Those stoves can be killers.'

'I will,' I promised.

* * *

Five weeks later Roger went to London to pick up our plane tickets.

'We're going to Lebanon!' he shouted and waved the papers when he got back to the mill. I was so relieved.

'Casino Du Liban!' Roger laughed.

He seemed almost jolly, but then Roger's moods could change at any moment. I couldn't bring myself to relax and laugh with him. Nonetheless the casino sounded exotic. I smiled. We were set to leave in a fortnight.

# Chapter Nine

We arrived in Beirut in August 1968. It was a city that had been under attack during the Six-Day War with Israel the previous year and the streets were still conflict-torn. Between the burnt-out buildings there was rubbish strewn everywhere and the pavements were dusty and dry. As we drove from the airport it was strange to see armed militia patrolling the city. Suddenly I became aware of what kind of place we were moving to. There were sirens going off and an atmosphere of general tension. People in the street stared at us in our taxi. I suppose they were wondering why foreigners wanted to come to Beirut at such a difficult time.

I pointed out the sights to the children. The Arabic buildings were exotic compared to everything they had known in Manchester, and the robes, hats and veils worn by the passersby looked to us as though they had come straight from a picture book. Jude, now aged three, stood on the seat at the window and pointed and asked questions about everything she saw, while twenty-two-month-old David quickly fell asleep on my lap.

'Where are we going?' I asked Roger.

'The apartment, of course,' he said.

He had told me nothing about the arrangements. I was just glad that we were no longer in the mill-house and had an apartment to go to. Peter had accompanied us on the plane and had an apartment of his own, so we dropped him off first.

A woman named Maggie, the ballet mistress at the casino, had organized a flat for us in the building where she lived. We picked the keys up from her. Roger put the suitcases in the tiled hallway and I walked around our new home. It was a very old, Arab-style apartment block. The rooms were square and the furniture was clean and tidy. We had a huge, ornate, balcony that looked out over the street and through the open door I could hear the sounds of Beirut life, including the call to prayer from the mosque nearby. Jude and David ran round and found their little bedroom with small twin beds and a cupboard. Up till now they had always shared a bed and they thought this set-up was hilarious.

'One for you, one for me,' David counted out.

'But I'll miss you all the way over there,' Jude giggled.

They were on a high. It was a far cry from the damp, rat-infested mill.

The ballet mistress had employed a nanny for us, called Marie. Her job was to look after the kids when I wasn't around and to help out around the flat as well. When we arrived she was waiting for us. Marie was dark and she had a solid air about her, as if nothing would phase her. I liked her immediately. Anyone in Beirut over the last months had probably been through a lot of upheaval and I realized that, with the war ending, this was a brand new chapter in Marie's life as much as it was in ours.

'*Salaam alechem*, madam,' she said.

'*Salaam alechem*,' I tried out the greeting, and Jude thought that was very funny. She ran round the living room repeating the words herself.

It was important to me that life in Beirut was as normal as possible for Jude and David. I knew the children of some other entertainers had to trail their parents to the late-night parties that were inevitable in our line of work but I was clear that I didn't want that for my son and daughter. I didn't argue with Roger. I knew that he never bothered much with the kids and that if I organized a routine and saw to it all myself, he wouldn't complain. Already this place seemed a huge improvement on the last: for a start, we had a nanny and a house with four walls. I was optimistic. It even crossed my mind that Roger might like it here and maybe he would be happier and easier to live with. The five years of our married life had been so dire to date that I thought 'Surely it can only get better?'

That first day I took Jude and David out for a walk to explore the neighbourhood. 'Where do you think the sea is?' I asked them. I knew it was a few blocks away, behind our apartment building, but I wanted the kids to figure that out for themselves. From the start I always encouraged them to be self-reliant. It was important to me that they felt confident in the world.

Jude looked thoughtful. There were seagulls wheeling above our head and she could smell the sea. 'That way,' she said decisively, pointing over her shoulder.

She was right. Clever girl.

We walked down the road, past a couple of stalls selling sweets and hot mint tea and I chatted to them, telling them about all the fun we were going to have here and that we could play on the beach every day. As we rounded a corner and saw the yellow stretch of beach and sparkling blue ocean ahead, David burst into an excited run.

The next day, having got the details from Marie, I enrolled Jude and David at the local nursery. It was a lovely place with a playground in the garden that was bordered by olive trees. The teacher, Mrs Kadshi, had smiley eyes and I saw straightaway that all the children adored her. That was the only recommendation I needed. There were classes every morning in both French and Arabic, which the children picked up remarkably quickly. This left me free to rehearse at the casino. Knowing the kids were happy was the main thing.

Then I turned my attention to the show. The Casino Du Liban was very glamorous and exotic and the show was spectacular. There were dancers and a variety of wild animal acts, including horses and dolphins, as well as the Globe. Mr Henchis's stage manager, Nigel, was there to welcome Roger and me when we first arrived. Peter came too. He shook my hand enthusiastically then he and his wife, Maggie, the woman who had organized our flat, gave us a guided tour.

Among the people we were introduced to was a blonde girl called Amy, who was getting made up in one of the dressing rooms. Nigel told Roger that they wanted him to train her to ride in the Globe so that she could be my understudy.

'I'll look forward to working with you,' Roger told her.

I remember feeling pleased, because training a novice would take up a lot of his free time so he'd have less time to spend with me and the kids. Everything was straightforward and I could enjoy my relationship with my children when he wasn't around, nagging, undermining and beating me.

The dance scenes were choreographed by Jack Cole, who had choreographed a number of famous films. He took the dance routine from the fight scene in *West Side Story* and adapted it for fourteen motorbikes – two gangs of seven. It was to be the headline act at the casino so it was important to make it a real stunner. The gangs roared in through the audience and Roger and I made our entrance as the stage split in two, revealing the Globe with us inside. It rose to stage level, lit up like a Christmas bauble, tantalizing the audience with the sound of bikes that they could not see. Then the lights were switched off leaving only a spotlight on the top plate giving the illusion that we were riding on air. It was very clever.

Charley Henchis arrived just as we came into the auditorium and seemed to be delighted with everything. Roger was excited as well; it was leagues more sophisticated than the show we'd been in at Belle Vue. I was pleased when Nigel told us the timing: the show started at ten o'clock and we weren't on until quarter to eleven, so I had plenty of time to tuck Jude and David in bed at seven and make sure they were asleep before heading off to the theatre. Maria would stay in the apartment with them, but I'd be there when they woke up in the morning. It was perfect.

We went backstage to get ready for a run-through. Charley had arranged a bizarre costume for me. The thrill of the act was that I was a woman doing this dangerous stunt, but riding at speed it would be difficult for the audience to make that out, so to hammer the point home he decided that I was to wear long, yellow PVC boots, teamed with a black mini skirt and yellow top. Even at sixty miles an hour no one would be able to miss me. I tried on the boots, but they immediately made me very concerned. The PVC wasn't quite tight enough around my thighs and I was worried that the vibrations from the motorbike might make them ride down, which would be dangerous.

I approached Charley and explained my problem.

'But we have to make it clear you are a lady, yes? Try it. Try it,' he urged me.

I didn't want to make a fuss. After all, we were earning a fortune and if I messed things up, God knows what Roger would do to me. I climbed into the boots and made a mental note to get the wardrobe mistress to sew some tight elastic round the tops.

'Break a leg,' Amy said, as I walked towards the under-stage lift that would provide Roger and me with our big entrance.

'Don't muck it up, for God's sake,' Roger snarled at me.

Then from somewhere in the wings, I suddenly heard a voice I recognized. It was more gravelly than I remembered but still distinctive and it immediately stirred up a memory of my life in South Africa. I turned to see a tall chap wearing a safari hat. He was silhouetted against the lights at first but when he turned towards me I recognized a familiar face, completely out of context in Beirut. I couldn't believe it.

'Carl!' I shouted, overwhelmed with delight.

'Judy! What are you doing here?'

He was as flabbergasted as I was. I hadn't seen Carl since I was eleven and ran away to the Wilkie's Circus. He had found me hiding out in a horsebox and took me under his wing. I'd helped him to tend the animals at that circus – horses, elephants, chimps, lions and tigers, camels and llamas – and he became my protector, one of the only true friends I had in those dark days. Surely this was a good omen.

Carl flung his arms round me. 'You're all grown up!' he said. 'Look at you!'

'Yes, but I'd have recognized you anywhere. What are you doing here?'

'Training the animals.' Charley Henchis had obviously travelled the world looking for the best circus professionals he could find, and that's why Carl ended up in Beirut at the same time as me. I was overjoyed to see him again.

Roger was immediately suspicious when I introduced them and I could see he was running every possible scenario in his head.

'I met Carl when I was a little girl,' I told him.

'She's a real gymnast, your wife,' Carl said generously.

Roger's face was a picture.

Then, it was time for us to go on. It was nice to be performing again. That night we did the show for the first time and the audience exploded into applause. As I took my bow I felt fantastic, though I was still nervous about those boots. During the performance I could feel them beginning to slip and I had only just managed to stop them rolling down.

All in all, we settled in well but Roger quickly adopted a Jekyll and Hyde act that was hard for me to swallow. In public, he had made it. He was the star of the show at the casino and was having the time of his life. If anyone needed help, Roger would step in and offer his assistance. Anyone, that is, except me. Behind closed doors, his campaign of threats, intimidation and violence continued unabated. The only difference from life in Compass Street was that now no one else was allowed to witness his brutality. My every move was analysed and Roger's outbursts were erratic and violent. It felt very dangerous. No-one, I was sure, would believe me if I told them about his behaviour towards me because it was completely at odds with his public face. I didn't want to threaten the fledgling friendships I had made in Beirut by causing a drama so I felt very alone once more.

Maybe I could have talked to Carl, but Roger made a point of befriending him despite the fact that he clearly felt threatened by him. To Carl's face, he was a fun-loving mate with whom to go drinking and partying, but back home he quizzed me relentlessly about 'what had gone on before'. No matter how often I explained how young we were in South Africa and that Carl and I had only been friends, Roger wouldn't give up. Whenever Carl came to visit Roger was charming but afterwards he would make pointed comments and insinuations and threaten me. The fact that he befriended Carl made me feel even more isolated, as he had sidelined one of the few people I could trust. Sometimes I took the children to visit Carl during the day and they loved to watch the circus animals being put through their paces. But Carl was friends with Roger and I never had the confidence to confide in him about the appalling treatment I was suffering at home. He was never aware of it.

Every week Roger took both our wages and told me he was paying them into a joint account. We were earning £58 a week between us and living in Beirut was cheap so we should have been saving plenty of money. I was happy for him to look after our finances and give me an allowance to pay the household bills but still he insisted on seeing receipts for everything. He complained about the cost of the nursery school and Marie's wages and questioned every single penny I spent. If something couldn't be accounted for he went crazy.

'You bloody thief,' he shouted, when I hadn't managed to get a receipt for some food I had bought from a street stall. 'What did you spend that money on? What are you planning?'

On the occasions when I couldn't get a receipt for something I worried myself sick, terrified of what he might do in his rage.

In the main, though, we lived separate lives. I stuck to my routine with the children. They got up early and I put them on the bus with Marie to go to the nursery. They came home at lunchtime then we spent the afternoon on the beach or at the souk. After bedtime I sneaked off to the casino. Marie did some housework and stayed with them until I got home. It was always late when I fell into bed and before I knew it, I was up again and serving breakfast.

Roger had a very different time of it. There were parties every night and he usually didn't get home until dawn. The way it worked out we saw less and less of each other. For me this was by far the best way but Roger was frustrated that I was thriving independently and he clearly wanted to assert his authority whenever we were together, which most days was only at work.

'You're not as good as you think,' he snarled as we made our way to the cage. 'I could mow you down any time I like. I could kill you, you know,' he threatened.

I knew he was right. He was in charge inside the Globe and I had to follow his lead.

At first these threats were idle and a more immediate concern were Mr Henchis's favourite yellow PVC boots. I continually had a hard job trying to keep them up for the whole of the show. It was very difficult riding with precision accuracy while having to grasp and grab to keep the silly things in place. I'd had them altered but the vibrations of the bike soon stretched them and the minute I got on, they began to creep down. I brought it up once more with Charley, but he was adamant that they looked great and had to stay, at least until after the World Press Review.

'Everyone will be there,' Charley gesticulated vaguely to indicate the enormous amount of people who would be present. 'King Hussein of Jordan will be there,' he said. 'The World Press Review is vital.'

'All right,' I agreed. But I was not happy.

The night of the Press Review the atmosphere backstage was electric and excitement at the casino was palpable. The whole building had been painted and spruced to perfection, everything checked and double-checked. The staff had been briefed on how to address the King. Everyone was ready. I pulled the boots on in my dressing room. I don't know if it was warmer that night and it had made the material more stretchy or if I had lost a little weight from all my rushing around. Whatever had happened the boots were even more loose on me.

'At least it might be the last time I have to wear them,' I thought and resolved to talk to Charley again as soon as the show was over.

Up in the cage we began to ride. I was acutely aware of Roger's bike, as he was of mine. You have to get into a rhythm together so you can perform as one. We began to circle and I felt the boots slipping down just as it was time for the most difficult stunt: Roger was to loop over me as I rode round the centre band. Full concentration was needed. I had to listen to the engine revs and be aware exactly where Roger was in the cage. Just at that moment the boots rolled down completely and ended up round my ankles before I could grab them. In an instant, the unguarded bike chain snapped up the material and twisted it into a tight rope that dug deep into my calf, binding me to the bike. The bike choked, the engine stopped, and I slid dangerously down to the base of the Globe. Roger was about to loop over me and he just had time to snake out of the loop and avoid a collision. If we had crashed, the bikes would have exploded on impact. We could both have died.

I don't think the audience realized what had happened. The next performers came on immediately. Nigel the stage manager had seen the accident, though, and he lowered the Globe below the stage as fast as he could. My leg was still trapped by the tight band of PVC material and it was throbbing ominously. Charley rushed from the auditorium to see what had happened and he cut me free with a penknife. I thought I was going to be sick from the pain as I bent over to check the damage. The skin wasn't broken but there was a deep groove running round my calf that went right down to the bone and the whole area was rapidly bruising.

Roger came over. 'What the hell did you think you were you doing?' he snapped.

Charley looked at Roger strangely but didn't say anything. He handed me gently to one of the backstage helpers and went back to the Press Review.

'Judy, I'm so sorry. You tried to warn us about those boots,' Nigel fussed. 'Do you think you can still do the finale?'

'I'll try,' I said.

I was very shocked but somehow I managed to carry on. A stagehand tried to patch me up, binding my leg with a dressing, which consisted of a poultice made of Arabic bread. At this stage I think I was on auto pilot. I got in place for the finale, which involved sitting on a chandelier and being lowered onto the stage while the dancers did their routine. The extent of my injury hadn't sunk in at that stage and somehow I managed to wave and smile as usual.

Next morning, though, the shock had dissipated and I was limping terribly. The pain was excruciating and I had to ask Marie for extra help with the children. It was clear that I wouldn't be working for a while, but I just tried to focus on how to look after the injury and on making sure the kids were all right.

'Jesus,' Roger muttered. 'You can't bloody do anything right, can you? Amy will have to take over, God help her.'

Over the next few days my leg deteriorated. I started having heart palpitations and was sure I was going to pass out. Finally, I got a cab to the local doctor's surgery.

'You need medical attention immediately or you could lose your foot,' he told me bluntly. 'I'm sending you to the hospital now.'

Luckily one of the female dancers from the casino had a car and she offered me a lift. On the ward they said that the injury was cutting off the circulation to my foot. Fluid was building up under the skin and my leg had become infected. The doctor made a diamond-shaped cut to drain the fluid. It was a deep wound and needed to be dressed.

'You need constant medical supervision,' the surgeon said. 'This could easily turn gangrenous.'

\* \* \*

When I got home, Roger was completely unhelpful. He had started to train Amy to do the act and he was out with her most of the time. For a while I had been suspicious about the way he acted around her and convinced that his interest was more than purely professional, and round about this time I got the impression that they might be starting an affair. To be honest, if his being with Amy meant that I didn't have to endure all his sexual fantasies, I was extremely relieved. I just had to concentrate on getting my leg to heal.

Roger pointed out that my visa was no longer valid when I wasn't working so I had no right to stay in the country any more. It was clear he wanted me out of the way so he could concentrate on his affair with Amy.

'Where should I go?' I asked, half delirious with the pain in my leg.

The truth was that the best option was back to Britain – at least I would get proper healthcare there. I suggested that I should rent a place back there for the short term but Roger wanted to be in full control of me, no matter where I was. The idea of me renting my own accommodation was completely unacceptable. He swung furiously into action and arranged with his mother that she would take us in if he sent money for our keep.

'Please don't make me stay there,' I begged.

But Roger held the purse strings and that was that.

'So my family isn't good enough for you? Think you're going to go swanning off on your own and expect me to pay for it? Well you can forget that! You're staying put at my mum's until the contract here is finished.'

My heart sank. Roger's contract was for the duration of the show, which in effect meant that he would be in Beirut indefinitely. I realized that he just wanted rid of me. He wanted to spend all his time with Amy and my presence was inconvenient for him.

I dreaded staying with the Lethbridges even for a short time but my leg injury was seriously in need of medical attention and with no money I didn't have much choice.

'OK,' I thought, 'I'll go back and let's see what happens.'

So I sprang from one trap right into another.

# Chapter Ten

As the plane took off from Beirut airport I felt a weight lift from me. It was a relief to know that we wouldn't be living with Roger for a while. I even dared to think that perhaps this was my chance to get away for good. Looking after Jude and David was my greatest pleasure and to be able to enjoy that without worrying about my husband and his constant threats and mood swings felt fantastic.

The kids were simply excited to be going on a plane. They seemed to have no qualms about leaving behind our life in Beirut and being so far away from their father. The truth was that Roger was a very small part of their lives. He hardly saw them.

Back in England the doctor prescribed antibiotics and dressed my wound. Within a couple of weeks it was getting much better and I was able to walk without pain. However, right from the start, it was awkward staying with my parents-in-law. The Lethbridges' house had only three bedrooms and there were still eight of Roger's siblings at home. I felt awkward taking up a bedroom for Jude, David and me, even though I knew Mrs Lethbridge was glad of the money that Roger was sending her. Financially I could see that she was struggling. Mr Lethbridge had lost his job and was on the dole so even with contributions from the couple of older kids who were working it was difficult to provide for everyone. Many evenings she served up boiled eggs for dinner because that was all she could afford.

I began to see where Roger's paranoia about women came from. Mr Lethbridge sniped at me constantly and was always nagging at his wife, claiming that most of the ten children weren't even his. Worst of all, he had his eyes on me in a predatory way. He kept appearing behind me, touching me and wanting to kiss me. I worried that maybe it was a test, and that he would tell Roger about it. We were at such close quarters in that packed, tiny house that it was impossible to avoid him so eventually I threatened to tell his wife about it.

I'd just put the kids to bed and came out onto the landing. He appeared from nowhere and pinned me in a corner, his hands on my chest and his breath in my face.

'If you don't get off me right now, I'm going straight downstairs to tell your wife,' I hissed, anxious that the kids shouldn't overhear but determined to get the message across.

'You wouldn't dare,' he sneered. He tried to slide a hand up under my skirt and I managed to grab his wrist and wriggle out of his way.

The harassment still didn't stop, though, with him grabbing at me whenever he could, so I decided to pluck up my courage and follow through my threat.

It took a while before I managed to get Mrs Lethbridge on her own without any of the kids around, but one day when I was helping her to peel potatoes for dinner, I came out with it.

'I'm really sorry, but your husband has been ...' I hesitated, trying to find the right words, 'Harassing me. He can't seem to keep his hands off me and I don't know what to do about it.'

She carried on peeling the potatoes, with her back to me. 'You're not the first,' she said. 'You won't be the last.'

Where did that leave me? 'Would you mind having a word?' I asked timidly.

'Not that it'll make any difference,' she agreed wearily.

After that, Mr Lethbridge stopped talking to me completely and the atmosphere became unbearable so I decided to look for alternative accommodation elsewhere. I leafed through the local paper, but everywhere I rang immediately asked 'Where is your husband?' Today that sounds outrageous, but in 1969 it was simply the way things were.

After days of phone calls and what seemed like endless conversations with landlords and letting agents, I couldn't find a single place to rent for a woman on her own with two children. Every day the situation at the Lethbridges' place worsened. It was a catch-22 situation. If I found a flat I could set us up a proper life and begin looking for a job – but finding a place was well nigh impossible.

'Right,' I thought. 'I'll just have to try harder.'

I decided to go to the bank and withdraw some money. Perhaps if I offered a larger deposit in cash I might have more luck. For months now I had been earning my wages at the Casino and apart from the meagre housekeeping allowance that Roger doled out to me, I hadn't seen a penny of it. Now I needed that money.

Mr MacKenzie, the bank manager at Barclays, looked apologetic when I was shown into his office. He was a kind man with a nervous habit of playing with his pen. That day it was spinning between his fingers as I explained my situation.

'The thing is,' Mr MacKenzie said slowly, 'that this bank account is in your husband's name. You don't have any money lodged with us. Technically, that is,' he added.

'But I've been earning almost £28 a week,' I said.

'That may be the case, Mrs Lethbridge, but we can't give you this money. It is your husband's, you see. It's in his bank account and you need his signature to make a withdrawal.'

My stomach turned over. Roger had told me that the money was going to a joint bank account. A blaze of fury surged through me. How dare he? It was just the latest and by no means the most serious of the cruelties he had imposed on me but for me it was the last straw.

My mind was racing. In the UK, even with my trapeze and circus skills I couldn't earn enough to set myself and my children up independently. Any salary I made would be eaten up paying for childcare and the idea of staying at the Lethbridges' long term was unthinkable. Roger clearly believed he'd sent me back to a situation where I would be stuck, and in that moment I realized there was only one way I could get out. My husband wouldn't give me money willingly so I would have to go back to Beirut and work at the Casino again, but this time I would build up savings in my own name. Once I had enough, I could start a whole new life without Roger. My rage about the theft of my money made me determined.

I appealed to Mr MacKenzie's better nature, being as persuasive as I could. 'I've got two young children with me and we need to get back to Beirut to sort this out. Please, please can you give me something?'

He bit his lip and spun the pen between his fingers. 'I do feel sorry for you. I am sure your husband wouldn't want you to be in this position.'

Mr MacKenzie had clearly never met Roger. There was an awkward silence as he deliberated and made his decision. 'I'm afraid I can only give you £100,' he said.

I almost collapsed with relief. One hundred pounds was a lot of money in those days but it was still going to be tight for paying for a journey for three of us from Manchester to Beirut; it wasn't nearly enough for three flights. I went to the travel agent and managed to organize an itinerary. The trip would take us from Manchester to London by train, then a ferry crossing to France, another train journey to Italy and, finally, a boat to Beirut. It would take ten days and by the time I'd bought everything we'd need, the whole journey cost me £98 so I only had £2 left over to pay for food during the trip. The survival skills learned in my childhood were certainly going to be a valuable asset.

I bought a flask, some tins of condensed milk, coffee powder and a couple of packets of cereal for the children, and I also made up several packets of ham sandwiches. The day we set out, the kids were excited. They had always enjoyed travelling and as long as I was with them they took everything in their stride. Now we played games about going back to Beirut to explain the complicated journey we would be taking.

'Will we be going on another plane?' David asked. He was excited.

'A plane is about the only thing that we won't be taking!' I told him.

We said our goodbyes to the Lethbridges. I think it was a relief for them to have their bedroom back and it was

certainly a relief for me to be getting away from Mr Lethbridge and his oppressive comments and snide insinuations.
Despite that, I had had a taste of freedom and was determined that once I had stockpiled enough money to make
things work, I would get away again to somewhere better.

'I'll survive,' I thought. I always had.

The first leg of our journey took us to London by
overnight train. As we boarded our carriage I asked the
porter to fill my flask with hot water and I made hot condensed milk for the children and coffee for myself.

'Would you like a cup of tea in the morning?' he asked.

'Is it free?'

The porter nodded.

'Yes please.'

At six-thirty the tray arrived. To save us buying breakfast I used all the items off the tea tray along with the food
I had brought. I put cornflakes in the saucer and the cup,
one for each child, then poured over the fresh milk that was
supposed to be for my tea, and added some sugar. They had
to take it in turns to use the spoon and as they passed it
from hand to hand I drank some black tea to get myself
going.

Later that day, as we waited at the port to board the ferry
to Calais, we sat on a bench, and I cracked open the ham
sandwiches. 'When we get on the train from Paris to Italy
we'll get dressed up and have a big, slap-up meal,' I promised. It was going to be a long day from now till then.

We were all starving and looking forward to our proper
meal when we boarded the night-train from Paris. We
changed into our best clothes and walked along the corridor to the posh dining room on board.

Jude and David sat down cheerfully and put their napkins on their laps as I perused the menu. My heart sank. The full meal cost £5 and I didn't have anything like enough money.

'Could we please just order some soup?' I asked the waiter.

'Sorry madam,' he said. 'We only serve the full meal.'

There was nothing I could do. We'd just have to wait once more.

'In that case,' I sighed, reaching into my bag, 'could you please fill this flask with hot water?'

I apologized to the children. 'We'll have to wait until we catch the boat tomorrow.' We trudged back to our carriage where I made hot condensed milk again and we finished the last of the sandwiches, which were now curling up at the edges.

'We are going to eat tomorrow, aren't we, Mummy?' David asked.

'You are a very brave boy,' I told him. 'And we are going to have loads of goodies when we get to the boat. You'll see.'

Our passage on the boat included all meals. Once we hit Naples, we'd be home and dry, I thought. I watched the children sleeping, curled up on their bunk beds and my heart went out to them. I knew exactly what it felt like to be small and hungry. It's the last thing I ever wanted for my own children.

The next day, Naples was bright and bustling. There was a crowd round our ship and we cheerfully walked towards the people, an air of expectation building. I was hoping that we could board immediately and get settled. By now we were

ravenous. But our troubles weren't over yet. As we got closer I realized that many people in the crowd were holding
banners written in Italian.

I pushed to the front of the crowd with our tickets in one
hand, both children holding the other. There was a man in
uniform at the top of the gangway.

'We apologize,' he said, 'but our crew are on strike. Come
back tomorrow.'

I was flabbergasted. 'Tomorrow?' I repeated, trying to
take it in. I had hardly any money in my purse – where was
I supposed to stay, with two children, until tomorrow? And
what were we supposed to eat? The prospect of a night
sleeping rough in Naples filled me with horror. I could have
managed on my own, of course, but not with a three-year-
old and a four-year-old in tow.

Jude just stared. She was a stout-hearted little thing but
I could see she was upset. David held her hand. We hadn't
had a proper meal since we'd left Manchester almost three
days before. It wasn't good enough.

'Right. Come along, you two,' I said, drawing myself up.
'I'm going to sort this out.' Having the children to look
after made me brave. People had messed me around in the
past and I hadn't been good at standing up for myself, but
now I had the responsibility of protecting them and that's
what I was going to do.

We walked back down the gangway and I hailed a taxi on
the dock. I asked the driver to take me to the head office of
the shipping company that owned the boat. I was determined that we were going to have a proper meal that
evening and somewhere safe to stay. As far as I was concerned, the shipping company had let us down so it was the
shipping company that should put things right.

I marched the children into the office and asked to see the manager.

'He is very busy,' the secretary said.

'That's fine. I am a passenger on your ship that is stuck at the dock. I have plenty of time. We can wait.'

A few minutes later the manager emerged. I think the secretary had realized that I meant business and wasn't going anywhere. The man approached me apologetically. He clearly hadn't expected to have to deal with disgruntled passengers himself and was caught on the wrong foot.

'Hello,' I said. 'I have a ticket here that says your ship leaves on Tuesday 19th February. That is today. It is unfortunate that your crew have decided to go on strike, but I have no money and nowhere to go. What are you going to do about it? We have travelled here from far away and your company has let us down.'

'But *signora* …'

'But *signora* nothing. This is no way to treat your passengers. If need be I'll sleep in your office. I am not taking my children out of here until something is done. You can't just sell tickets that promise full board accommodation and then not provide it.'

The manager looked as if I had slapped him in the face.

'I had to come here in a taxi which is still sitting outside because I can't afford to pay the driver,' I said. 'You have to help us.'

The man sighed. My words had hit home, though. 'Go and pay this lady's taxi,' he instructed his secretary and then he reached for the telephone. 'I'll see what I can do.'

Half an hour later we were booked into a nearby hotel. That evening, all dressed up, we went to the restaurant downstairs and ordered huge bowls of minestrone soup.

The kids gulped it down appreciatively and Jude even told me it was the best meal she'd ever had in her life.

'Food always tastes better when you're really starving,' I told her.

It was a massive relief for me. Seeing Jude and David hungry was a painful reminder of my own childhood. When I was their age, Freda used to shut me out in the back yard all day long and hunger pains would gnaw at my stomach. I didn't have water either and sometimes my thirst was so great that I was forced to drink from the bowl of the outside toilet. The idea that my children would ever be short of food was deeply distressing to me. I wanted things to be completely different for them.

After dinner the children spent most of the evening bouncing on what was the largest bed that any of us had seen. I sat and watched, cheering them on until it was time to go to sleep.

The next day the captain said that passengers could return to sleep on the ship, but there would be no other services as the crew were still on strike. He gave us a small allowance to buy food – 1,500 lire, roughly £1.50 for the three of us, which ultimately had to stretch over three days.

Seeing the money in my hand made me remember the tips I had stolen from restaurant tables in South Africa when I was homeless many years before at the age of twelve. Even a little money can be a great treasure, I thought to myself. And I knew that I'd make it last.

Every day we found a new adventure. We visited parks, shops and found a local market. David was a blond, good-looking child and the Italian stallholders were enchanted with him.

'*Bambino, bambino,*' they cried enthusiastically and pinched his cheeks.

Sometimes they pressed an orange into his little hand or slipped an apple into his pocket. This was a godsend.

'*Grazie,*' he learned to say, and then handed the fruit to me so we could divide it up later.

Often, a trip through the market meant three or four oranges and after we'd wandered through the stalls we feasted in the shade of the trees in a nearby park. Every evening we ate soup or pizza with the money provided by the cruise company. On the third day the boat sailed and I still had a little bit of English money left that I had kept aside in case things got really dire.

Several days later, nearing the end of our journey, I stood on deck and watched Cyprus recede into the distance. Beirut was our next port of call and as a celebration I bought the children Italian ice cream at the ship's verandah café. By that time there was only one shilling left in my purse, but I felt safe enough to spend it. We were almost there.

'Come on,' I took the children downstairs into the passengers' lounge where there was a jukebox. I popped the shilling into the slot and pressed the number.

'Listen to this,' I said.

The Beatles had just released the single 'Hey Jude'. It blasted out over the speakers and Jude's face broke into a huge grin.

'Let's dance,' I told her. 'You, young lady, have a song.'

# Chapter Eleven

I had written to Roger to tell him which ship we were arriving on. He replied, saying that he'd come to the dock to meet us. We stood on deck and searched the crowd on the dockside for any sign. Jude pointed excitedly.

'There's Daddy,' she said. But it was someone else.

The kids liked Beirut and were looking forward to going back to Mrs Kadshi's nursery and playing with Marie. They chattered happily as I wondered how I was going to get to the casino without any money.

After an hour, when almost all the other passengers had disembarked, I asked the porter if he could get us a taxi.

'My husband must have been held up,' I said to the taxi driver when he arrived. 'Can you please give the porter his fee and then add it to your fare?'

He kindly agreed and went to sort things out.

It was a twenty-five-minute drive to the casino. When we got there, it was still quite early in the day and George, a Polish acrobat, was the only person I could find. I explained the situation to him and he kindly paid the taxi for me.

'Roger isn't here,' George explained without meeting my eyes. 'I'm not sure where he is. I will go and have a look.'

My senses were acute. Something was definitely wrong. When George came back a few minutes later he looked contrite.

'He's at Amy's,' he stammered. 'I'll take you there. Let me help you with the bags.'

George clearly thought I would be upset but, of course, the affair came as no surprise to me. In fact, I was hoping that it would take the pressure off me, by keeping Roger out of my way. At Amy's apartment, George knocked on the door and we all entered. There was no one in the living room. The kids ran in. 'Daddy!' they called out.

Roger emerged from the bedroom. 'Judy!' he exclaimed. 'I didn't think you were coming today.'

'Well, we're here now,' I replied.

I saw a movement through the open door. Amy was pulling on a dressing gown and it was obvious she had just got out of bed.

'Hello Judy,' she said sheepishly.

'I've got us an apartment next door,' Roger started to tell me, but I was already heading for the bags. I just wanted to get out of there. It wasn't right in front of the kids. Roger pulled a key out of his trouser pocket and handed it over.

'That's fine,' I said and led the children across the hall.

Roger never did move into the other apartment with us. He stayed at Amy's every night. I hadn't come back to be with him, I'd come to get away but still, when I looked out of the window and saw their washing hanging up together on the line, it was a strange feeling. When I married him, I had taken my vows very seriously, including 'till death us do part'. It was obvious that I had to get away from him for my survival, but still I felt sad that I hadn't been able to make my little family work out. My dream was well and truly over.

When the children asked, 'Where's Daddy?' I made light of it. I wanted life to seem as normal as possible for them.

'He's fallen asleep at Auntie Amy's again, the silly billy,' I told them.

Every morning I made coffee and we all took it across to the other apartment so the kids felt that their Dad was still part of the household. It hurt, but it worked.

Meantime, I was steely in my determination. I was going to ride the Globe, make my money and then get out of there. Being back in Beirut only made me more determined. I'd had a few weeks without Roger in England and that had given me strength. I was set on regaining that feeling of independence again.

'Good to have you back, Judy,' Nigel shook my hand when I turned up backstage. Then in a concerned whisper he asked 'Will you be all right?'

'I'm fine,' I said. 'Really. I better go and see the boss, though, hadn't I?'

'My lady rider!' Charley boomed when I walked in. 'How is your leg?'

I grinned. '100 percent better,' I promised. 'I'd like to go back to work, Charley.'

That week I signed a new contract and this time it was in my own name.

'And you'll pay me directly?' I checked. 'Cash in hand?'

'Certainly.'

'And Charley, I'm glad to be back, but I want a pay rise.'

This time, poor Charley looked as if he was going to cry. He was a tough negotiator but I had him over a barrel. There was no other female rider who had the experience and skills that I had and I knew what a draw that was on the billing.

'All right,' he said and in the end I got £30 – as much as Roger.

Roger was clearly coping less well with our altered living arrangements. For the first few weeks, he mostly restricted himself to verbal abuse. Our schedules were very different – he and Amy slept most of the day and partied all night. He was enjoying being the star of the show and was very popular with the other performers. I only brushed up against that world and was never truly part of it. I slipped into the casino, did the act and came home to the children.

'You useless bitch,' he'd sneer when our paths crossed. 'You're nothing without me.'

I don't know how Roger found out about my pay rise but three weeks into the job, when he did, he went mad. As far as he was concerned it was the worst snub possible. He didn't see me as his equal and couldn't bear the idea that we were paid the same amount.

That afternoon, I was on the beach with the children and Peter when we heard Roger bellowing. He was charging along the sidewalk and it was clear he was livid. He belted onto the sand and grabbed me in a fury, viciously punching, slapping and screaming at the top of his voice.

'What favours did you give Charley then?' he spat. 'I suppose you think you're dead clever now?'

Every punch was agony and I was winded. Luckily, the children were with some friends further along the beach. I just hoped that they couldn't see what was going on.

Thank God Peter was there. He flung his arm around me and pushed Roger off. 'Leave her alone,' he shouted. 'You can't treat her like that.'

'You get your bloody hands off my wife!' Roger shouted, even more infuriated.

Peter stood his ground. 'Go on! Go and cool your heels somewhere else, Roger. Leave Judy alone!'

It felt good to have someone stand up for me and I was comforted by Peter's help. Roger was a coward at heart and, after a couple more insults, he skulked off.

'All right?' Peter asked.

I nodded. My skin was stinging. The attack had been vicious but it was over quickly and apart from a few bruises I'd escaped unscathed. My stomach was sickened, though. I knew in my heart of hearts that kind of fury didn't go away and that Roger wasn't finished. Mind you, even I hadn't reckoned on what he would do next.

That night I was nervous as I got to the casino. Sitting on my bike ready for the Globe to be raised to stage level I looked across at Roger. His eyes were narrowed to vicious slits and he stared at me with pure hatred. He looked slightly out of control. Surely, I thought, he won't try anything here. I knew how important his 'nice guy' image was to him. And there had been talk lately of the show going for a run in Las Vegas, which was something Roger definitely wouldn't want to mess up. But what if he hated me more than he wanted his job? Underneath my costume I could still feel the bruises from earlier.

When the music began we started the bikes and all my comforting thoughts went out the window. From the very first moment I realized that my life was in the hands of a mad man. As Roger accelerated he tried his best to knock against my back wheel. In the confined space of the Globe this was a death wish for both of us. My heart thumping, I dived to get out of his way, dodging all over the cage, testing my skills to their limit in an effort to stay clear of his bike. At the end of a very long three-minute ride, during which I could have died at any second, the Globe was lowered below stage, and Roger fell off his bike in a drunken stupor onto the bottom of the cage.

'Oh my God,' I breathed, shaking with shock. What was he doing getting into the Globe after he'd been drinking?

The Lebanese roadies who stowed the bikes away hardly looked twice as my husband staggered off, stumbling up the stairs.

I knew that no one watching the show would have realized what was going on – two motorbikes racing around a confined space 16 feet in diameter looks more or less the same, whichever way you ride it. But what Roger had done was terrifying. He wanted to kill me, there was no doubt about it.

That night in bed I scarcely slept as I relived every moment of that ride. It shocked me that Roger hadn't thought either of me or of any consequences for the children. He didn't even seem bothered whether he killed himself or not. His jealousy of my growing independence from him was overwhelming.

Things seriously deteriorated from there. Roger was angry all the time and though he'd always been threatening towards me now things escalated. Every night in the Globe he snarled in a drunken temper. 'You'd better keep out of my way, you useless bitch. I'm going to mow you down.'

I literally spent most of the act staying out of his way rather than doing the stunts we had rehearsed. It was terrifying, not least because he seemed to be drunk every night now. Even if he just meant to scare me, one slip could easily be fatal for us both. I knew I had to do something fast.

Initially, I had hoped I might stay in Beirut for perhaps a year and be able to save up a really substantial amount. That clearly wasn't possible now. I had to leave as soon as I could. Every day I stayed was pushing Roger further and further to the edge. Each night I left the stage numb with relief but terrified that I'd have to do it all again and knowing that my luck was bound to run out eventually. The thought of what would happen to the children if I had a serious or fatal accident left me sleepless and I racked my brains for a way out that would release me from my contract, give me a new life and wouldn't simply further infuriate my now-homicidal husband. I had to make a move soon – I wasn't sure how much longer my luck would hold out inside the Globe and Roger was getting so used to his daily round of deadly intimidation that he was almost becoming blasé about it.

It was lucky for me that Roger cared so much about his public persona. And the fact that Charley intended to take the Globe to America was a bonus. Roger was excited about that trip and I knew that he didn't want to jeopardize it.

One night, before we went on, I decided I had to make my move. It took a lot to stand up to Roger. Inside I was still the same little girl that my father had terrorized and beaten to within an inch of her life. My heart pounded and my hands shook. I drew in a breath and summoned all my courage.

'I think that it would be best for the kids and me to leave Beirut,' I told him.

'You think you can do whatever you want, don't you? If you leave I'll bloody well come after you, don't think that I won't.'

I had to hold my ground. Besides, it was an empty threat. Roger loved to ride. The truth was that if I left he wouldn't come after me. That would break his contract.

'Roger,' I said steadily, 'if you don't let me leave I'll go to Charley and I'll tell him everything. Everyone will find out what you're really like.'

I could see Roger considering this. There was a lot at stake. Right now, no one knew about the constant threats and my nightly terror in the Globe. I don't think anyone else was aware quite how much he was drinking, apart from the Arab stage hands who saw him nightly as he flopped, inebriated, from his bike at the end of the act. Roger would have hated it if I had blown the whistle on him and in his drink-addled state I could see this paranoia flash through his eyes. I recognized how that felt. Roger was thinking 'I could lose everything.'

'You blackmailing piece of shit. You can't tell me what to do.'

I stared him straight in the eyes. He must have been surprised at the change in me. I'd hardly ever so much as answered him back before now. 'You don't need me,' I said. 'You're going to Las Vegas. Charley won't bring a rider who's caused a big accident. Only the best for the Americans, Roger. I think it would be a good idea for the kids and me to leave Beirut.'

'You'll never manage on your own,' he snapped.

'Is that what you think?'

I could see that he was grappling with his ego. He hesitated for a moment. 'You're a slag and a whore and you think you're too bloody good for me,' he snarled. 'Well, you're nothing. You're not worth the shit on my shoe. I'm not going to let you get in the way of the Vegas run. So fuck off, why don't you? Who cares?'

'Good. I was hoping you might organize the tickets,' I said. 'You at least owe me that after all the money you pocketed from my wages.'

'Hah!' he laughed and then he thought for a moment. I held my breath. It was difficult for women to organize travel tickets in Lebanon so this was important. Roger loved to be in charge and an arrangement where he bought me tickets gave him leverage. I think the idea amused him.

'OK, I'll organize tickets but only if you tell Charley you're quitting because you've lost your nerve,' he said with a glint in his eye. He relished the thought of me admitting to what he saw as a weakness. Instead of grassing him up to Charley, I'd have to grass up myself.

'I'll do that,' I said. It didn't matter to me one iota.

'Well, you'd bloody better,' Roger snarled. 'Bloody coward. Back to Blighty. Useless cow.'

'I want to go to South Africa,' I said decisively.

After those few weeks in the UK I was all too aware how difficult it was to find accommodation in England as a single parent. In South Africa it was different and I knew it would be possible to get a nanny to help with the kids and that I'd be able to find a decent job in Johannesburg. However nightmarish my childhood had been there, I wasn't going to let my past dictate my future. At least Johannesburg was familiar; I knew my way around.

We stepped into our places to be lifted up into the Globe.

'South Africa? Well, that's if you make it through tonight's show,' he growled. 'Wonder what the odds are of that?'

As we rode in circles that night, Roger kept close to the back wheel of my bike. Knowing his instincts were addled by fury as well as alcohol was terrifying. It would only take his wheel to kiss the back of my bike and we'd be hurled into a petrol-soaked and bloody pile of flesh and machinery at the bottom of the cage.

'Please let me get through this,' I willed myself, my hands sweaty with terror as I rode as hard as I could. It was difficult to tell where Roger was and without seeing him at a safe distance I couldn't know each and every second whether it was my last. Every revolution of the cage brought another opportunity for him to threaten me, to chance his luck.

'Please. Please,' I begged.

And then, at long, long last the lighting changed, we pulled up in the base of the cage, the machinery cranked us below stage and the act was over.

As we descended, Roger turned to me again. I drew myself up on the seat of the bike. I didn't want him to see how scared I was. He was sitting nonchalantly, as if nothing had happened. He looked at me.

'You take Jude and I'll have David,' he said.

It was like hearing an echo across a very wide chasm. Here it was, exactly what had happened to me, taken away from my sisters because my father wanted to hurt my mother. Despite the adrenaline rushing through my system, or maybe because of it, my terror disappeared.

'Absolutely not,' I said.

I had never denied Roger anything quite so flatly, but there was no way he was splitting up the kids. That was something I'd fight to the death for. When he saw how adamant I was he realized he'd met his match. For a moment, he looked stunned.

'You bleeding watch it,' he said. 'Don't get cocky.'

But he didn't bring up the idea again.

As I left to go home to the children Roger was climbing into a taxi. I knew he'd stay up till dawn drinking and smoking hash. He caught my eye and leaned over to kiss Amy, then he looked up to see if he got a reaction. He didn't. I got into a taxi of my own and leaned back in the seat.

'I'm lucky to be alive,' I thought, still wondering if I'd get away with my next move.

It took Roger a deliberately long time to organize the tickets. I think he was dilly-dallying just to keep me dangling. On my side of the bargain, I didn't waste any time. Almost the next day I told Charley that since my accident I had lost my nerve and was too afraid to ride, and could he please release me from my contract. I wasn't sure how this would pan out. Charley didn't want me to leave because he couldn't readily replace me.

'Are you blackmailing me for more money?' he asked.

'No,' I shook my head.

'You don't want to go to America?'

'I'm too scared, Charley.'

He looked at me uncomfortably. Charley never liked dealing with women and I could see that he didn't entirely believe that I had lost my nerve but nonetheless, he shrugged his shoulders and ungraciously allowed me to leave.

I didn't have many friends at the casino. Carl had left while I was in the UK and I didn't even know where he'd gone to. Because I didn't attend the all-night parties I was never really part of the social scene that thrived around the show. One of the Canadian dancers, Rena, used to meet me sometimes for mint tea and she came over to the apartment to say goodbye along with another girl, Marian, who had given me a lift to the hospital the day I'd discovered the infection in my leg. They brought a box of delicious Arab pastries, which we ate on the balcony.

And then, at last, after weeks of waiting and enduring Roger's seemingly unending criticism and abuse, he finally produced the tickets. I was immensely relieved. We were to fly via Egypt and Kenya, and then on to Johannesburg. I had only managed to save £90 but that would have to be enough. Amy hovered in the background as I packed, while Roger drank steadily.

'You'll be back, you'll see. You can't do without me,' he snarled as I ushered the children into a taxi.

'Goodbye Daddy!' they trilled, excited as ever to be going on an aeroplane. They were still too small to grasp the fact that we weren't coming back and because Roger was never very involved with them it wasn't on their minds.

'I won't miss you one bit, Roger Lethbridge,' I thought. 'I've got my ticket and I'm off.'

As we drove away a wave of relief hit me. Roger and Amy were waving from the front of the apartment building and I looked back at them as they grew smaller and smaller. I had survived.

'This is the last time I'll ever see them,' I thought. I wanted to shout for joy. Instead I gave each of the children a tight squeeze.

'We're going to have a big adventure,' I said.

I'd done it. I'd got away.

# Chapter Twelve

$I$t was July 1970 and Beirut airport was packed. Israeli bombing raids against the PLO had started and many Lebanese had decided to flee the fighting. There hadn't been any shelling where we lived or near the casino but some parts of Beirut had become dangerous and there was a mass evacuation. At the airport most flights were full, there were queues for everything and some people looked as if they had been camping in the departure hall for days, waiting for a ticket to become available. Our ticket to Johannesburg took us to Cairo first and then Nairobi. We had a long journey ahead of us but I was so glad to be getting away that it didn't phase me in the slightest.

I fought through the crowd to the check-in desk, hauling the children behind me. 'Three for Cairo,' I said, handing over the ticket.

The stewardess was flustered and distracted. There was mayhem all round us, fights breaking out as people found they couldn't have what they wanted. She processed our tickets without really looking at them and only took a cursory glance at my passport. 'Through to the lounge. Gate 3,' she said.

As we passed through security the crowds got even worse. There was a long queue for the toilets and the café had run out of food. I loved the smell of the strong, Arabic coffee, though, as it wafted from the stall. Many flights were delayed because there was so much pressure on the system and each gate seemed to be serving at least two full airplanes. There were passengers everywhere.

'I hope it will be different when we get to Cairo,' I thought.

Our flight was running late, but only by a couple of hours. I sat with Jude and David and told them stories about Egypt – the sphinx and the pyramids and Cleopatra and her red-sailed pleasure ship on the Nile. I relished the fact that we were leaving Beirut for the last time. It felt like I had all the good things in my life with me and I'd left all the bad things behind.

Eventually the flight was called. It was overbooked. I gave up my seat for an elderly Lebanese lady and the children had to sit on people's laps. Everyone was anxious to get out of Beirut, and because many people were standing in the aisles, the air hostesses couldn't get through to serve drinks so we had to do without. When we eventually landed all the passengers cheered.

Cairo airport was much calmer. The children were getting tired. We checked in again and were told to take our bags through to the luggage counter.

'Just wait a moment, madam,' the man there said as he checked our papers.

He disappeared and came back with two customs officers. Neither of them appeared to speak much English. The woman gestured for me to come forward and the man picked up our bags. We were taken into a back room.

'Excuse me, but is there a problem?' I asked.

The woman motioned for me to sit. 'Stay here,' she said.

Then as the customs officers left the room they locked the door.

I didn't want the children to be frightened so I told them stories about a mummy who travelled with her children in a magic suitcase. They went all over the world and they were now on their way to Africa. I told them about African game animals – about lions and monkeys and zebras. David wanted to know if he could go and see them and I said yes, in the holidays we could.

We were stuck in that customs room for eight hours with nothing to eat or drink and only once did the woman come in to let us use the toilet. A huge clock on the wall ticked really loudly. I asked several times what was happening but she only shrugged her shoulders and said in broken English 'Please, this way.' I had no idea why we had been locked in and I was very worried. 'We'll miss our flight,' I said.

Then, inexplicably, after eight hours two officers came into the room. They didn't ask any questions, only took us back to our bags, which had been thoroughly searched. Everything was strewn about and some ornamental camels I had brought had been slashed open leaving sawdust everywhere. I wondered if they had thought I was carrying drugs?

'Pack your cases and get back to the departure gate,' the official said, pushing me towards the table where the cases lay open. He gave me my papers and then shoved us into the queue. I had no idea what the delay had been about. I was so glad they were letting us go that I didn't argue or make a fuss. I just wanted to get out of there.

The night flight to Nairobi took off on time and we all had seats. I was relieved to be getting on our way and put the rough treatment down to the fact we had come from a war zone. I began to relax as the hostesses moved round the cabin serving sandwiches. It had been a tiring day and it wasn't long before both children were out for the count.

It was exciting to be embarking on a new life and one where I could take the initiative and make my own decisions. Despite the traumas of my past life there, I was convinced that South Africa was a good choice for us all. I looked at the children, fast asleep in their seats, heads touching, and I felt an overwhelming rush of love for them.

In Nairobi we disembarked and made for the ticket desk. It was much too early to check in for the next flight but after the trouble we'd had in Cairo I decided to be on the safe side and check that all was well for the last leg of our journey.

'We're going to Johannesburg,' I said as I handed over the tickets.

'Sure,' the girl smiled but then, as she read the papers, her expression changed to one of concern.

'Could you please wait here for a moment? I have to show this ticket to my supervisor.'

After a while the supervisor arrived and I sensed immediately that something was wrong. 'I'm really sorry to have to tell you this, but there's no flight with this number. I'm afraid this ticket is a fake and has obviously been bought from a racketeer.'

My heart turned over and a tingle of intuition buzzed at the back of my brain. Could this be why we'd had all that trouble in Cairo? Was it because Roger had got his final revenge by buying us dodgy travel tickets? Sensing my shock, the supervisor kindly guided me to a comfy chair.

'My name is Ruth,' she said.

'Judy.'

'Where did you get this ticket?'

'My husband bought it in Beirut,' I said flatly. 'Please,' I entreated her. 'I can't go back there. I need to get my children to Johannesburg. We're starting a new life.'

Ruth nodded. 'I understand,' she said gently. 'Let me see what I can do. I'll just go and make a phone call.'

Ruth disappeared into an office behind the check-in desk. I felt sick. I knew that the ninety pounds in my purse wasn't enough to buy three plane tickets and set up a new life in Johannesburg. Why did everything have to be so flipping hard?

I kept replaying the events of the last few weeks. The long wait for Roger to get the tickets, the treatment at Cairo airport and the echoing retort of Roger's parting speech, 'You'll be back. You can't do without me.' I had the creeping realization that perhaps this was what he had meant. I felt a wave of horror. Surely they wouldn't send us back? A vision of Roger with a sickly smug grin on his face appeared in my mind's eye. Yes, maybe he knew this was going to happen. In fact, he probably hadn't reckoned on us getting this far. I hoped desperately that somehow things would work out and that the long shadow cast by Roger's cruelty wasn't going to ruin our chances of starting over.

Ruth eventually returned waving an envelope. She scribbled something onto a pad and then passed it to me. 'I'm going to try to pull some strings for you. I have arranged for you to be dropped in town for the day,' she said. 'That's the name of a café. Go there this afternoon at five. My boyfriend works at the airline headquarters. He will come and pick you up and bring you back here. You're so obviously a genuine case, I'll see what I can do.'

'Thank you so much,' I said, taking the piece of paper.

I had never been to Nairobi before and God knew what Ruth's boyfriend might be like. It did occur to me that this could be some kind of elaborate set-up but I looked at Ruth and decided that I trusted her. To be honest, I didn't have much choice.

'I'll be there at five,' I promised. 'Thank you.'

Ruth's friend dropped us right in the city centre. Nairobi was bustling. Jude and David loved the sights. They had never been anywhere with a black population before. The brightly printed dresses and head scarves African women wore were very different from the black smocks worn by most women in Beirut. There were children selling oranges at the roadside and, between the modern office buildings, there were shacks with corrugated roofs that served as shops.

I saw a small, dusty-looking park and took the children to sit on a bench.

David wanted to know if there might be any monkeys around so I explained that it was unlikely in a big city but he should keep his eyes peeled all the same. I bought some fresh mangos from a stall and we had a picnic. There wasn't much else to do.

We walked around the centre for a while. I saw a sign for a museum but we couldn't find it. I kept the children's spirits high by pointing out the different kinds of trees and letting them look in the shop windows. Jude had some money that one of the dancers at the casino had given her when we left. We went into Woolworth's and she decided to spend it on a little, red-haired doll that she christened Diane.

It was a tortuous day. My mind was in constant turmoil. Here I was stranded in a strange country with my two children and with no sensible way out. All the time I kept thinking 'Where are we going to sleep tonight? What's going to happen to us?' I was isolated and had put all my faith in Ruth, someone I'd never met in my life before. At half past four we headed for the café. My heart was pounding.

Nervously checking the time, I took a seat outside on the pavement and ordered the children a fizzy drink to share. 'I need to stay focused,' I told myself. 'Just stay calm.'

Then I heard a cheery voice behind me, 'Hello, are you Judy?'

I turned and a tall, African guy with a friendly face was standing behind me. I nodded.

'I'm Marcus, Ruth's boyfriend.' He held out his hand to shake mine.

'You guys better drink up. I'm going to take you back to the airport.'

He led us over to his car. I was on full alert. I didn't know this guy and now I was getting into his four-by-four with my children. Every nerve in my body was jangling. The children were oblivious.

'Does Marcus hunt lions in this car?' David turned to me and asked.

Marcus laughed. 'Not so much,' he said. 'But I did see a giraffe last weekend.'

I sat in the back with my hand on the door handle, just in case I had to grab the children and run.

When we got to the airport Ruth was outside. She came rushing towards the car waving a piece of paper. 'I've arranged with Olympic Airways to fly you free of charge,' she smiled.

I was so relieved I almost cried. 'What?' I could hardly believe it. 'That's fantastic! Thank you so much, Ruth. You've saved our lives!'

When they'd heard our story from Ruth, Olympic Airways had stepped in and offered us the tickets. I have never forgotten that generous hand of friendship in our hour of need. For years afterwards whenever I needed to buy plane tickets I always chose to fly with Olympic. I don't know what I would have done without their kindness that day.

'There are some genuinely good people in the world,' I said to myself. I laid a blanket over my sleeping children while we jetted south that night. What I didn't recognize at the time was that my instincts for discerning good people from bad were beginning to get stronger. It was a long process but at last I was learning how to judge who I could trust in the world.

When I woke up we were landing in Johannesburg and the sun was rising.

# Chapter Thirteen

It was haunting and strange returning to Hillbrow, a residential area of Johannesburg that in the 1970s under the apartheid system was designated 'whites only'. I had lived there for eighteen months when I was about twelve, surviving somehow on the streets after my father abandoned me, moving home without telling me where he had gone. I slept in a shack behind a liquor store, eating whatever I could find and washing in the public toilets at the local cinema or swimming pool. A decade later, it had hardly changed at all – just a few more bars and clubs had sprung up – and the sight of a familiar turn in the road could send me spiralling back to harsh memories of starvation and desperation. I pushed these thoughts to the back of my mind as much as I could.

Hillbrow was also a place where I knew my way around and for that reason it was comforting. The fact I had survived made me all the more determined to tread those streets again with my head held high.

When we first arrived, I was edgy and apprehensive at the thought of meeting my father. I was no longer afraid of him, but I would not have wanted to come face to face with him again for the first time since I left South Africa eight years before. I knew his very presence would strip me of my confidence. Even though I had survived his years of tyrannical abuse, the effects of it hung over me like an evil shadow every day. He'd left his mark good and proper but as far as I was concerned he'd done enough damage. I ventured into the local spiritualist church to make enquiries and was told that he'd been hissed off stage one night and booted out. He'd left Johannesburg for the far-away province of Natal, and I knew he would be too proud to return so that was a weight off my mind. Now I truly had the chance of a new start and was going to make the best of it. My children and I were free, and ready to face the world.

During those first weeks I found a flat and enrolled Jude and David in pre-school. While they were there I went to business college to train to be an accounts clerk and soon found a job in a woodwork factory earning 170 rand a month. This was not a fortune but I was able to live cheaply and, like most white families, afford a nanny. Rosa was a fat, black grandmother with lots of experience. The kids liked her and I felt comfortable leaving Jude and David in her care for the few hours before I got home. Things were panning out well.

Because of my low income I qualified for legal aid so I applied for a divorce from Roger as soon as I could. I sat in the lawyer's office under a buzzing fan. The lawyer, Mr Saga, was a very efficient but gentle character with a mop of pure white hair and piercing blue eyes.

'Where can we contact your husband, Mrs Lethbridge?' he asked.

I gave the address of the casino in Beirut. Mr Saga's eyebrows raised.

'His occupation?' he asked.

'He's a stunt motorcyclist.' More raised eyebrows.

'Well,' Mr Saga said slowly, 'in this case you will require an international divorce which must be notarized in the High Court in London.'

'How long will it take?

'Perhaps two years,' he said with a serious air.

'Can we start straightaway?'

That autumn Jude was old enough to go to school but unfortunately the only school in the area was the primary division of my old school, Barnato Park. I had had a terrible time as a senior there. Dad had never bought me the right uniform or books and every day there was some humiliation lined up for me in class. Once I had to stand in front of the other children at assembly as everyone took turns to criticize my scruffy appearance, and the headmistress even lifted my skirt to show that I wasn't wearing the regulation black knickers. The teachers had no understanding of my home life and every tiny rule had to be adhered to – for them a matter of discipline but for me, completely in my father's control, the harsh repercussions were devastating.

I was glad that the junior and senior schools were separate so I didn't have to come into contact with any of my old teachers from those days. I was determined that Jude would have everything she needed so I saved up carefully to buy her uniform and all her books. I was so proud seeing her off on her first morning in her crisp white dress and hoped against hope that her schooldays there were going to be happy ones. The place hadn't changed, though, and it wasn't long before I realized that the same niggardly attitude prevailed as it had in my day.

Jude was an excellent swimmer and was chosen to represent her team in the school swimming gala. She was in a house that had green as its colours and I was told she had to have a completely green towel for the big day. I searched Johannesburg for days looking for the requested pure green towel but I could only find one with a green and white pattern on it. On the day of the gala Jude was told she wasn't allowed to swim because her towel was not regulation. She was made to sit and watch from the sidelines. I was absolutely furious. This was exactly the sort of thing that had made my life such a misery only a few years before and I wasn't going to have it. I marched into the school building and demanded to see the headmistress.

'Does it really matter about the colour of a towel?' I seethed. 'Can you not see that here is a child who has something to offer and you have punished her over some stupid, minute detail. Is this the way you treat the children in your care?'

The headmistress barely looked at me. 'This is Barnato Park,' she said, 'and that is how we do things here. We are teaching your daughter to be disciplined, Mrs Lethbridge.'

'My daughter doesn't need to be disciplined,' I snapped. 'She needs to be encouraged.'

It was no wonder that Jude didn't enjoy school from then on. Nonetheless, we fell into an easy routine. Barnato Park finished at 1.30 pm every day so Rosa picked up Jude from school and cared for her until I got home after work with David, who I collected from his nursery. I thought things were going well.

One Friday afternoon, as David and I walked home we chatted about what we would all do over the weekend. Jude had had a small accident the day before and had a large bump on her forehead. I had taken her to the hospital and although there were no problems the doctor had advised a day of rest from school just to be on the safe side. Rosa promised to watch closely over her until I got home, and luckily we finished early on a Friday so she wouldn't be waiting for very long.

We let ourselves into the flat and almost immediately I could tell that something was wrong. Usually Jude ran up and gave me a big hug and tripped over her words as she spilled out all the news of the day. Today there was a deathly hush. I called, 'Jude, oh little Jude, where are you?' But there was silence. I walked into the kitchen because Jude often played a game where she hid in the big cupboard and then jumped out at me, and as I did so I saw Rosa pick up her bag. Before I could talk to her she swiftly left through the kitchen door, mumbling 'Bye, Madam.' My senses were now on full alert. This was unusual behaviour. We always discussed that day's events and on Fridays we made plans for the coming week.

'Jude, where are you darling?' I called again. Just silence. I went into the bedroom and there she was. Her face was white and her large brown eyes were filled with tears as she sat silently on the bed hugging her knees to her chest. 'What's wrong, sweetheart,' I asked as I pulled her onto my knee. 'Tell mummy, why are you crying?'

Jude rested her head on my chest and sobbed quietly. David came and sat next to his sister and held her hand. 'What's wrong, Jude?' he asked, full of concern, but Jude couldn't speak.

My mind was working overtime. Whatever could this be? It must have been something huge because this was so unlike Jude. I knew how difficult it could be to open up about some things. I was an adult of twenty-five years old now but I still couldn't tell anyone about the traumatic things that had happened to me as a child. I just sat and held Jude and stroked her hair, waiting for her to find the strength to tell me in her own time.

Finally, she lifted her head, looked me in the eyes and, as the tears fell, she said, 'A man took me in the flat downstairs.' My blood ran cold, and for a moment I couldn't breathe.

'What happened then, sweetie?' I asked as calmly as I could.

She began to cry more openly and said through her sobs, 'He took off my pants and hurt me.'

The room span and I thought I might pass out, but I held her tight. 'Not again, not to my child,' I was screaming inside my head. I remembered vividly what it felt like to be hurt and abused. A memory hit me full force. I was eight all over again. The deckchair man was pushing me down hard onto the sand. I was struggling with all my might. I could feel his weight crushing me, the sand on my back. The sour, horrible smell of him. His grunts as he forced himself inside me. And the deep, dark pain.

I fought the panicky feelings brought back by the memory, fought my panic for Jude. Had it been the same for my precious little girl? My thoughts were jumping all over the place as Jude explained to me that she had been left alone in the flat and was bored so she went out to look for someone to play with.

'No-one was home,' she cried, 'and it was a man who does the cleaning that took me downstairs.'

'Where the hell was Rosa?' I thought grimly. I'd put my trust and faith in that woman. How come Jude was left on her own? What in heaven's name had been going on?

'What do you remember about him?' I asked gently.

'He smelled of polish and he wore bright yellow shoes.' The man had clearly terrified her because she was shaking like a leaf as she asked, 'Will he be here tomorrow?'

My heart raced as memories of my own experience swamped me. I'd been terrified for ages that the deckchair man would come back and attack me again. I'd had to survive that trauma totally alone, but Jude had me to look after her. I had to swallow my own feelings for now, appear calm and in control, and not fall apart.

'I'm going to sort this out, Jude. That man has to be punished for what he has done. He won't hurt you again. Let's go and see the superintendent.'

The superintendent of the building lived upstairs so Jude and I went up and knocked loudly on her door. We had never actually met properly before but she was genuinely shocked to hear what had happened that day. Her concern was evident. A worried look crossed her face as she said, 'I am sorry but the law is very clear. I have to report this at once. It's an assault on a white child by a black man.'

I was very apprehensive about Jude having to face a police enquiry. I really just wanted the cleaner fired immediately. 'She's only five years old,' I said. 'To involve the police ...'

The superintendent touched my arm and said, 'I am so sorry, but it is the law.'

Things moved very fast after that. The police arrived and took a statement, and a forensic team went to work in the flat downstairs where the assault had taken place. They removed the carpets for tests and I was ordered to take Jude to the hospital to be examined by a police surgeon. I was flabbergasted. To me this was a further assault on my little girl. I couldn't imagine what it would have been like to be examined after I had been raped. I had been so disgusted already that another stranger touching me down there would have been an abhorrent thought. But there was no choice; the police were adamant she had to go through with it.

At the hospital Jude was taken into an examination room by a very large police surgeon. 'You will have to wait outside,' he told me sternly. Had my daughter not been through enough already?

'Forget that,' I replied 'I'm staying put.'

The examination was deeply traumatic for Jude. Having to undress and have a strange man examine her was more than she could bear. She struggled to get off the bed and I could only kneel beside her and hold her as close as I could. The examination proved that there had been a grave attempt to rape her, but because she was so small it had obviously been difficult.

I felt sick to the bone thinking about it. Who could do that to a five-year-old girl? I couldn't wait to get Jude home and I carried her on my back all the way. After I tucked her into bed that night, a senior officer came round and prepared me for the next step of the investigation.

'Tomorrow we will have an identity parade. Do you think she'll be able to pick the bastard out?'

'Yes, she's absolutely clear. She knows who it was,' I said.

I was not happy about all this. Involving the authorities was completely alien to my way of dealing with things because in my own childhood whenever social workers or policemen had been brought in, things had gone from bad to worse. I was now treading on unfamiliar ground. I had no idea of how legal systems worked. As ever, I felt very much on the outside. I had an uneasy feeling about it all.

'We always prosecute in these cases,' said the policeman.

I had no understanding of what a trial of this nature entailed and nobody stepped in to explain things fully. I simply assumed that if I had to do anything they would let me know. That night I barely slept. I was filled with a fiery mixture of emotions – utter and complete revulsion at what had been done, devastation that I had been so badly let down by Rosa, and a profound well of sorrow for my little girl. My own instinct was to remove the man from the building and care for Jude myself from then on. I just wanted her to recover from all this and I was deeply concerned that an investigation and a court case would only serve to keep the memory alive.

'Perhaps when he is convicted it will be good for her to see that the system protects you,' I tried to convince myself. But in my gut, I was mistrustful. Either way, it wasn't up to me. The case was going ahead and we'd have to get through it as best we could.

# Chapter Fourteen

*N*ext morning, the police got all the cleaning boys in our building to line up on the roof. Sixteen men in their early twenties stood against a white wall. There was no protective viewing screen. They told me that Jude had to stand in front of them all and make her choice in full view.

'We need Jude to do this alone, without you there,' the officer told me.

'But she's only five,' I protested.

'She has to do it without being coerced in any way. You keep well away and we'll call you when she's finished. We need to be sure.'

Finally I agreed to wait on the stairs, while the superintendent and a police sergeant took little Jude up on her own. I'd explained to her what she had to do and she was quite matter of fact about it.

Jude picked out the man immediately. He was still wearing the shoes she remembered, which were bright yellow. The police officers changed the line up again, and she chose the same man. Finally they called me up and once more Jude pulled the same man out of the line.

'Kaffir cleaning boy!' the policeman exclaimed as his colleagues took him down to the waiting police van. 'We've got him now.'

Jude had identified him three times to different officers.

'Will he be in custody now?' I asked.

'Yes, pending the trial'.

That, as far as I was concerned, was the main thing. I explained to Jude that the man was being locked up and she didn't have to be afraid any more.

That afternoon after the police had gone I fired Rosa. She stared at me pointedly but said nothing as she left. She never apologized for what had happened or explained fully why Jude was left alone in the compound whilst in her care, but I suspect she had gone upstairs to have a chat with a friend of hers who had a room at the top of the building.

'We'll find another nanny,' I promised the kids.

This, however, proved very difficult. In the South Africa of the 1970s any interaction between black and white had a political slant. Word spread that I had fired Rosa and that the police were bringing a case against the cleaner. In the eyes of the underground black freedom movement I was a white woman discriminating against the black community. No one wanted to work for me. I was blacklisted. I had never heard of a white nanny in South Africa so if I couldn't recruit a black woman from the townships my childcare options were limited.

To me, the accusation that I was racist seemed crazy. All the time I was homeless in South Africa I was outraged at the way the black community was oppressed. I had often been mistaken for a black girl myself as the sun deepened my skin colour so I had seen it first hand. The second time

I was raped, when I was twelve, it was by a white man who thought I was black. I hated apartheid and all it stood for. I shrugged my shoulders and hoped that somehow we would get back to normal but it was a forlorn hope. For the rest of the time in Africa, things would never be the same again.

As we waited for the case to come to trial a campaign of intimidation began. An animal skull was left outside the door of our apartment. I began to check the mail for tampering and got nervous of noises in the night. There had been news stories about explosive devices put into cereal and soap packets by the servants in white homes so I knew the threat was very real and I had to be fully on my guard. I became acutely aware of everything going on around me but at the same time I had to try and hide my nerves from the children so as not to scare them.

The evening before my twenty-sixth birthday I decided that we all deserved a treat. I loved spending time with the kids, going for outings or planning something indulgent. That night we went for ice cream in an open-air restaurant in Hillbrow where I used to steal food left on the tables when I was homeless fourteen years before. It felt good this time to be able to pay my bill and leave a nice tip for the waitress.

It was Jude and David's bedtime when we got home and they were tired climbing the stairs. Flicking on the light, I said 'Right you two, off to bed,' but then I stopped in my tracks. Our flat was completely empty. Blank white walls stared back at me as I surveyed each room. Every stick of furniture had been taken. There wasn't a single thing left – not a cup or a sock or a bar of soap. It was only when I went into the bedroom that I saw my bed was still there. It was a heavy old thing and they hadn't been able to move it. Apart from that the place was a shell. They had got in through the balcony at the back of the flat and had stripped the place completely. All we had was what we stood up in.

My first thought was 'Thank goodness we were out when this happened.' Robbery in South Africa could be a brutal business and the papers were full of stories of people who had been beaten or even murdered when their homes were broken into. At this time 'necklacing' was prevalent. A tyre was placed around the neck of the victim (who was usually white) and then set alight.

'Looks like we're camping tonight!' I said to the kids as I ushered them inside.

'What happened?' David asked, clearly bemused.

'Sometimes bad people come and take things that don't belong to them.'

Jude sat on the floor and crossed her arms. There had obviously been too many bad people of late. I scooped the children into my arms and gave them both a big hug.

'We'll sort this lot out in the morning,' I said. 'Now the main thing is that you two go to bed and get some sleep. You have school tomorrow.'

I borrowed some blankets from the superintendent and we made up my bed while she fixed the lock on the balcony, where they had got in.

'I didn't hear a thing,' she told me. 'And I was right upstairs.'

It was unnerving for everyone.

Very late that night the superintendent knocked on the door. She handed me a kitchen knife. 'Thought you'd like to have this,' she said. 'You never know.'

'Thank you,' I said gratefully and slept with it under my pillow.

The next morning I went down to get my lift to work. Jack Graham, the firm's accountant, lived further along the road and every day he picked me up on his way to the office.

'Where's the cake then?' he asked cheekily as I opened the car door.

It was the tradition at work that if it was your birthday you brought a cake for everyone to share. We had been joking the day before about whether I'd bring chocolate cake or not – Jack was a real chocoholic – but I had completely forgotten about it. Jack could see I was upset. He stopped the engine and put a hand on my arm.

'Hey, what's the matter Judy?'

'I was burgled last night,' I said. 'They took everything, Jack. There's not a stick in the place.'

'Oh my goodness! Don't you worry,' he promised. 'We'll get something sorted out.'

Everyone at work was horrified at what had happened and they had a whip round. At the end of the day Jack dropped me home and unloaded the boot, which was full of bits and pieces people had donated to help refurbish the flat. Last of all there was a small chocolate cake with four candles on top, packed in a white cardboard box.

'That's for you,' Jack said 'To share with the kids.'

Their kindness touched me deeply. I felt so privileged to have such good, kind friends. It meant a lot to know there were sympathetic people on my side at a time when I mostly felt utterly alone in a hostile environment with responsibility for the welfare of my two young children.

\* \* \*

Waiting for the trial seemed interminable. During this time Jude had her sixth birthday but she was still very young to be testifying in a court of law. I was worried about how intimidating the court might be and over the weeks we chatted quite a bit about what would happen. I wanted to give Jude the confidence to open up.

'You will need to answer questions,' I said. 'And then they will punish the man for what he did.'

'How will he be punished?' Jude asked.

'He will go to jail,' I promised her.

'I'll tell them then,' Jude said stoutly.

I was so proud of her.

At last the letter arrived giving me the date of our court case – 14 June 1971. We were ordered to attend. I felt very relieved. At least it would all be over in a month or so. Now Jude could give her evidence and then we'd put what had happened behind us. I sat by the window and looked out at the dark, African sky and wished for Jude to stay strong. She needed all the support and strength I could give her and I was determined to be there every step of the way. I needed to keep looking forward because whenever I looked back at what had happened to her, and what had happened to me all those years before, I became speechless with the strength of the emotion. I couldn't afford to dwell on things because I needed to stay focused. It won't be long now, I thought, and then we'll be free of this for sure.

How naive could I be?

# Chapter Fifteen

The trial took place in a formal courtroom. I was shocked when I heard that Jude was expected to take the stand and give evidence like an adult. I knew how intimidating this would be and I was determined to ease her way as much as possible, so in the run-up to the hearing I tried to prepare her for what might happen and encouraged her to speak confidently.

'The judge needs to figure everything out,' I said. 'He needs to hear the story from everyone and then he tells us what he thinks.'

'And then does the bad man go to prison?' Jude asked.

'Yes, he won't be able to do that to a little girl again,' I told her. 'So what you say is very important. You might only be small, but everyone will be listening to you.'

'OK,' she said, bravely.

The day the trial started I took Jude to the courtroom. It was agony having to hand her over to the police officer who would take her to the waiting room until it was time to give her evidence. I hoped there might be a female custodian for her but instead it was an enormous male officer in uniform.

'Now remember everything we talked about,' I hugged her. 'I'll be in the courtroom, watching out for you.'

As she disappeared down the corridor without a backward glance, my heart ached.

Sitting in the courtroom waiting for the trial to begin, all I could think of was Jude. Soon it would all be over, I told myself. I just hoped she would be all right. It had been a difficult time since the robbery. I was constantly on my guard against intimidation from the underground freedom movement and I read each day's newspaper aghast at the violence that was going on all around us. I still slept with the kitchen knife under my pillow every night, ready to defend my family at any moment. Now here we were in court, my daughter about to give evidence. This trial would see us vindicated and then we could go back to a normal life. It was all I'd ever wanted.

A few minutes later the cleaning boy was brought into the dock, wearing overalls that had clearly been issued to him in custody. He didn't seem the least bit nervous and adopted a cool, detached expression as he stared at everyone coming into the courtroom. I tensed up. How would it be for Jude seeing him again? I felt physically sick looking at him.

Once everyone had taken their seats, she arrived. A policeman led her to a box on the other side of the podium from her assailant. She looked very small from where I was sitting and the ledge at the front of the box came up to her nose. 'My lovely little girl,' I thought. However much I had tried to bolster her confidence I knew that seeing that man again would scare her. I hoped her courage would hold.

Then the defence lawyer took his place. I drew myself up; I knew that we had truth on our side. Surely that was what the institution of justice was all about? As the judge took his seat, we settled down to business.

First of all, I was alarmed when the court noted that there was no lawyer representing Jude. This was my first encounter with South African law and all its implications and procedures, and the upshot was that I simply didn't understand what was going on. The legal system had failed to inform and advise me about our rights, and after the initial investigation there had been no support from anyone. The only communication I received from the courts was the subpoena to attend. I naively presumed that it was the court's responsibility to represent the victims adequately. A flicker of panic crossed my mind. Was this all going to go horribly wrong? I put it out of my mind – after all, this was about justice and Jude had right on her side.

The police officers testified that Jude had been resolute in the identification of her assailant. She had pointed him out on three separate occasions on the day of the identity parade. The forensic evidence was also compelling. According to the experts who testified, the carpet had been taken from the downstairs flat and after examination it was confirmed from the semen samples found on it that a sexual assault had taken place. The police doctor testified as to what his examination of Jude had found, and the superintendent of our building also testified strongly in our favour.

Then it was Jude's turn. As she cast her eyes around the room I saw her gaze linger on her assailant. I caught her eye and nodded to show my support. Then the lawyer defending the cleaning boy asked her to explain what had happened on the day of the assault. His tone was aggressive and he asked complicated questions again and again, clearly trying to trip her up. I was horrified at his manner. It was no way to deal with a little girl who had just turned six, never mind one who had been so brutally victimized. The superintendent, who was sitting on the other side of the courtroom, stared at me with her eyes wide open as if to say 'What on earth is going on?' The couple who lived in the flat where the assault took place also stared over at me, the man shrugging his shoulders as if to say 'How can they talk to a child that way?' It took all my strength not to jump up and make an objection.

Jude didn't falter, though. She ran through all the details with courage and confidence. In a way it was worse hearing my daughter tell her story in this environment and under attack from the defending lawyer than it had been on our own at home. The facts were stark and she stuck to them. When she was asked to identify the man who had touched her she pointed firmly toward the man in the box.

'That's him,' she said. 'He's there.'

The defence lawyer questioned every one of her answers trying to trip her up, but Jude stood firm. I was so proud of her but so upset on her behalf. This was a grim and intimidating experience for such a small child but Jude shone through it.

Now it was the assailant's turn to be questioned. I noticed immediately that the tone of the trial changed. This man simply wasn't put on the spot in the same way Jude had been.

'Where were you in the building that day?' the judge asked him.

'I was downstairs cleaning a flat,' the man said.

'And did you see the young lady on this side of the courtroom?'

'No. I didn't. I didn't see her all day.'

Jude jumped up. She couldn't bear the fact that the man was lying. I'd told her to speak up for herself and now she did.

'That's a lie! He's lying!' she said.

'Miss Lethbridge,' the judge rebuked her, 'please be quiet.'

'But he's lying!'

'So after you'd cleaned that apartment, what happened?'

'I saw her playing with my brooms and brushes outside.'

'So you did see her?'

The man looked confused.

'And did you speak to her?'

'No.'

'That's a lie too!' Jude chimed out and then, poor mite, she burst into tears.

I couldn't bear it any longer. I rushed up to the witness box.

'Mrs Lethbridge,' the judge said, 'this is most irregular. You cannot enter the witness box.'

'Try and stop me,' I snapped. 'My daughter is upset.' I put my arms round Jude.

'It's not right,' she sobbed.

'Mrs Lethbridge, you cannot stay in the witness box.'

'I'm staying put,' I said.

The judge looked perturbed, but he realized that I was not going to leave Jude to stand alone any more so he relented. Jude gripped my hand.

'Did you go up to this young lady at all?' the judge continued with his questioning.

'I passed her on the stairs. She was on her own.'

'So you did go up to her?'

'No.'

From my new vantage point I could see everyone's faces. The superintendent of the building and the people who lived in the flat downstairs were astounded at this performance. The man had now calmly changed his story three times and no one seemed to be picking up on the fact he was contradicting himself. After the grilling that Jude had been through this was definitely not fair. I had a distinct feeling that something was going horribly wrong but there didn't seem to be anything I could do. The judge was doodling haphazardly on a sheet of paper, obviously bored by the proceedings.

'So you didn't assault this young lady?'

'No sir.'

'You didn't have contact with her on that day?'

'No sir, not me.'

In the end the judge took less then ten minutes to make his decision.

'Please rise,' he said, and the defendant stood.

Jude was looking at me.

'This is a difficult case. There has certainly been an assault here, that evidence is clear. But I cannot take the testimony of a six-year-old child that it was this particular boy. I have no alternative but to find the defendant not guilty.'

I was stunned. The words rang in my ears. Jude continued to stare up at me, not understanding what was happening. As the assailant was led away he cast us a snide look. I felt my anger well up and I just wanted to get my daughter out of there.

'Come on, Jude,' I said and pulled her quickly out of the courtroom.

'What the hell was that all about?' our superintendent started to say as we passed, but I couldn't talk. I was too angry.

'But Mummy …' Jude said, realizing slowly what had happened as we came into the street. 'He lied.'

'I know, sweetie.'

'I told the judge what happened. I told the truth. Why didn't he believe me?'

I didn't know what to say to her. It was soul-destroying. I crouched down and hugged her tight.

'I'm sorry, Jude,' I said. 'That judge was wrong. I am so sorry that he didn't believe you, but everyone else does. And you know you told the truth. That's all that matters.'

As we turned to go I heard running footsteps behind me. It was the cleaning boy's lawyer.

'Mrs Lethbridge,' he called, out of breath. 'I am so sorry. I was the defence lawyer and even I couldn't see how he could get off. They've made a right pig's ear of this one.'

'Sorry just isn't good enough,' I turned on him. 'No child should ever have to go through that. You were brutal. And now he's got off. Maybe the next six-year-old that gets attacked might not be alive to tell you the truth.'

'I know. I am so sorry.'

Tears were rolling down Jude's cheeks and I knew it would be difficult for her for a long time. To have spoken up and not been believed would feel almost as damaging as the assault itself.

I picked up my daughter. 'Let's go home, sweetie.'

There was nothing more to say. I couldn't begin to verbalize the outrage I was feeling. Somehow we would just have to get through it together.

# Chapter Sixteen

I rocked Jude to sleep that night. I couldn't explain adequately what had happened and why she hadn't been believed. It was a harsh experience for such a small child. Worse still, with no conviction to keep him away, Jude's assailant was able to take up his old job in our building. There was no alternative. We had to move.

House hunting was difficult with two small children. I still hadn't managed to engage a nanny and so I was juggling childcare and favours all over the place. At work they were wonderful and arranged for the office driver to pick up the children and then bring them to me in the afternoon.

'Any time you need a few hours off that isn't a problem,' Jack Graham said.

I don't know how we would have managed without his kindness and understanding.

I was still very much on edge. I was terrified that, emboldened by his experience in court, the cleaner might try to assault Jude again and I didn't trust anyone to look after her at home in the afternoon. When I confided this fear to one of my colleagues at work, she suggested that I phone the education department about their assist-ed placement scheme. It was there to help families in cri-sis and if this wasn't a crisis, then I didn't know what was. Assisted places were offered at boarding schools on a temporary basis to give a family time to get out of a difficult or vulnerable situation. I applied and was suc-cessful, but was devastated to learn that the only place available was in a school two hundred miles away in Petersburg.

I had a difficult decision to make. Emotionally, it was the worst time for us to be separated when Jude needed the comfort of her mummy right there by her side. She was still very upset, but in the end I decided her safety had to be paramount. I couldn't risk that cleaner coming after her again. I would send her to the school, but only for a few weeks until I found a new home for us to live in.

As I packed Jude's things into a case I explained it all to her. Jude eyed David, who was playing in the corner of their bedroom. I knew what she was thinking.

'David is too little to go with you,' I said gently. 'He'll miss you.'

Jude drew herself up. 'Will you be able to come and see me?' she asked.

'Definitely.'

She wrapped her arms around my neck. I was anxious that she would be lonely. I had spent three years in an orphanage run by nuns between the ages of four and seven and I hated it. Now I was sending Jude away to an institu-tion simply because we were under such a dreadful threat that I feared she wasn't safe at home. The way her experi-ences kept throwing up echoes of my own past was very hard to deal with, but I had to keep reminding myself that it was different, because she had a parent who loved her while I hadn't had anyone.

Dropping her off at school broke my heart. It was a nice place with lots of amenities and the matron, Mrs Skop, had an easy smile but I was still worried leaving my daughter in her care. It was very difficult to walk back to the train station knowing that Jude would fall asleep in a dormitory that night. I had hated the coldness of communal living when I was that age so I was determined to bring her home to me again as soon as I possibly could.

My financial situation was very strained despite the bursary for Jude's care, and it was difficult to find an affordable new home anywhere near my work. I viewed lots of houses and apartments but they were all far too expensive. Near where we lived there was an ex-pats club called The Britishers' Club and I sometimes took David to play with the other kids there. They had a noticeboard so I put up a little sign asking if anyone knew of affordable accommodation.

One afternoon I took David to the club to watch a kids movie while I worked my way through the to-let ads in the paper. A shadow fell across me and as I looked up there was a tall, dark-haired guy smiling down at me.

'Hello. I'm Max,' he said.

We shook hands and the first thing I noticed how loose his grasp was.

Max explained that he was flat-hunting too. He had recently moved from the UK to take up a job as an engineer in a large bakery and was sleeping on a friend's sofa until he could get a place of his own. He had such a calm and placid demeanour that I immediately felt at ease in his company.

'How about we flat-hunt together?' he offered. 'I've got a car.'

This was a boon as I had only been able to look at a couple of properties a day at most when travelling between them by bus.

'Thanks. That would be great,' I said.

It didn't take long for me to realize that Max was extremely indecisive. While I had the constraint of a low budget and needed a home suitable for family living, Max had only himself to consider. We viewed several bachelor flats and small apartments that would have suited him fine but instead of making any kind of decision, he dithered and floundered.

'What do you think?' he'd plead. 'Do you like it? Tell me what to do.'

After two or three weeks of stressful viewing I was becoming desperate and to help us relax Max offered to take me to a social evening at the Britishers' Club. The place was buzzing and it was a real party atmosphere. We got chatting to two friends, Ann and Dave, about our difficulties in finding anywhere and they came up with a solution I hadn't considered before.

'Why don't you team up and house share?' they suggested.

After much consideration I decided that this might be a good solution. Max seemed a really nice, gentle guy and he was great at playing with David. House sharing was very common at that time, and between us we could easily afford a nice, three-bedroom house in a reasonable area. Best of all, it meant Jude could come home. I agreed that we could start looking together.

This was Max's first trip away from home. Up until then he had lived with his mother. There was only a couple of years difference in our ages but our experience of the world was poles apart. I had lived all over the world and learned to be streetwise from a young age. Max had been mollycoddled all his life and simply wasn't good at dealing with practicalities. I found his mild demeanour comforting and after my brutal relationship with Roger, Max's reliance on me made me feel safe. I didn't want that to be misunderstood, though.

'If we do this,' I said to him when we were on our own, 'I want you to know that there is no romance to be had.'

'No, no, of course not.'

'It will be separate bedrooms and all of that,' I said.

'That's fine. Really.'

The following week we found a nice house on Adam Road in Boxburg. It was a good area, close enough to a decent children's school and to my work. We moved within a week. The first evening it felt strange when Max and I had dinner together, but soon that became normal and we fell into an easy routine.

That first weekend we all drove to Petersburg to pick up Jude and bring her home. She had only had to board there for six weeks, but I had missed her dreadfully. I knew how every day can seem interminable for a child in an establishment like that. Although the boarding school was a much warmer place than St Joseph's, the orphanage I'd been in, I hated to think that my daughter had been away from home in an institutional environment.

'We had baths together and the bigger girls washed us with soap. I didn't like it,' she said.

A shiver ran down my spine. Exactly the same thing had happened to me. I'd had to sit in a bath with the other little children while bigger girls scrubbed me roughly with a soapy flannel, and I used to panic and struggle when soap got in my eyes and mouth. I pulled Jude to me for a big hug, feeling awful that she'd had to go through something I'd found so traumatic. It was as if history was repeating itself again.

'You'll love our new house,' I told her in the car on the way back to Johannesburg.

Jude held my hand and buried her nose into me. 'You smell of Mummy,' she laughed.

Later, as I unpacked Jude's things in her bedroom it began to dawn on me that everything was working out. I certainly had a few blissful weeks that winter. Max was as good as his word and although I sometimes caught him staring at me there was no suggestion of romance. I looked after most of the practicalities and Max came and went like a lodger, joining in whatever we were doing if he was around. He asked my advice about every single decision he had to make and for the very first time my opinion was listened to and valued. I felt overwhelmed to be so appreciated.

After the winter, though, things took a turn for the worse. The consequences of the court case caught up with us again. The political situation in the country continued to escalate into disorder. We were still blacklisted and while the move had put the underground off our scent for a short while, it reared its ugly head again when one afternoon I found a couple of windows smashed at the end of the driveway. I became paranoid, checking the doors and windows twice in the evenings and sleeping fitfully. I was nervous of reporting incidents to the police after what had happened with Jude's court case – I wanted as little official attention as possible – but as the months passed, the incidents mounted up.

Max seemed very laid back about these attacks. The papers were full of far worse and everyone in the community knew someone who had been badly affected by the anti-white violence.

'Don't worry,' he said. 'It'll all blow over.'

I knew he was too easy-going. I felt increasingly tense and began to sleep with a knife under my pillow again.

Then one night we came home from a drive-in movie to find the house had been broken into. Our possessions were stolen and bloody handprints lined the walls, but worst of all Jude and David's hamsters were dead on the lawn. They'd had their throats cut. Both children stood frozen in the garden. Their faces were drained and they were clearly in shock.

'You two, go into the kitchen.' I directed them away from the carnage.

This time I did call the police and they sent a squad car immediately.

'Mrs Lethbridge, this is very serious. It's definitely a warning,' the officer told me.

'What are they warning me about?'

The officer shifted uncomfortably from foot to foot. He lowered his voice. 'It could be the children next.'

I felt sick and dizzy. Somehow I managed to get Jude and David to bed and once the police had finished taking photographs I cleaned up the mess. The months and months of intimidation had finally got to me and when Max came home I knew I had to talk to him about taking some decisive action.

'Now, now,' he said uncomfortably. 'They were only hamsters.'

'Max,' I said, 'I have to move. I'm going to find a new place.'

'That's fine. If you want to move, we'll move. You find a place. Just tell me where.'

As usual Max expected me to do all the legwork and make all the decisions although I was glad he wanted to come too. Perhaps if there was a man around the place it might act as a deterrent. The thought of poor, incompetent Max as a deterrent was amusing but then, how were they to know he was as meek as a mouse?

Within a few days I had found a duplex apartment in Knights Park, a few miles away. I was hoping for a new start. We'd have to move quickly as the black community was a close network and news travelled fast. Most households had black maids, nannies and cleaners. I became extremely wary of any black person knocking on the door or even loitering outside. I didn't trust any of them. On the last day at Adam Road, I packed our things into boxes and waited for Max to come home from work.

As we drove away from the house I turned to watch Jude and David sitting together on the back seat. It was three years since we had arrived in South Africa and they were now settled here. If only I could make them safe.

Max turned the car into the new apartment complex. I had chosen it specifically because all the apartments were grouped around a central square and from a security perspective I knew this meant our neighbours would be easy to alert if there was an attack. I took a deep breath and offered up a silent prayer. 'Please let us be OK here.'

# Chapter Seventeen

When we moved to the duplex Max changed his job. Up until now he had mostly worked the day shift but when the opportunity presented itself for a regular slot at night, he jumped at it. He was an odd fish and I knew that it appealed to him to be alone in the bakery with no one to oversee him.

This left me in a quandary. I was on my own almost every evening and was very aware that if anything untoward happened it would be up to me to take action. Every day I read the papers, horrified at the intimidation that other families were suffering. There were daily reports of bombs, murders and rapes. Our day-to-day life, by contrast, was quiet. I enjoyed my job even though the methodical accounts work was a far cry from the thrills and spills of my stunt riding days. Now we had moved away, I hoped that the troubles would pass us by.

Jude and David started a new school and made several new friends. Their best friend, though, was a stray black and tan mongrel who'd adopted us. He bore the scars of the road on him, so we called him Hobo. This was the first dog I'd had since poor Gyp, my best friend from the age of seven, who used to comfort me after Dad and Freda had beaten me up. It had broken my heart when Gyp was taken away, driven down the road in a van with lots of other dogs, just before we set off for South Africa. Now Hobo quickly became part of our family, sleeping on the balcony every night and becoming inseparable from the kids during the day.

It was important for us to get on with life and for several weeks things were fine, though I still slept with my trusty knife under the pillow. But one night a few weeks after the move, I was woken by the sound of noises on the roof. I jumped up and grabbed my weapon with my heart pounding.

'What the hell is that?' I whispered to myself.

It sounded as if there were several people above me and I could hear them moving across the roof. Then there was a sound from the hallway.

'Oh my God, they are trying to break in through the skylight.'

A sickening fear grabbed me as I stepped lightly across the bedroom and into the hall. I could vaguely make out the outline of their shapes in the darkness. I felt trapped and terrified. Every survival instinct I possessed was casting around desperately for some kind of salvation. If these men broke into the house I would have to defend myself and that was that. I looked around, trying to figure out where the best place would be to take them on. Should I hide? My fingers felt numb with terror and I grasped the knife as firmly as I could. Whatever I had to do, I'd do it. The fumbling on the roof was getting louder and I was frozen right underneath it, looking up.

They say that God moves in mysterious ways. That night our guardian angel was Hobo. He began to bark, making a hell of a racket and waking all the other dogs in the complex. Almost immediately lights went on in the square and as I looked out of the window I saw one or two of the neighbours come out of their front doors with guns in their hands. One of them fired a shot over the rooftop. I ran outside and saw three black men scurrying as fast as they could across the roof to avoid being identified in the bright lights. Hobo and the other dogs chased after them, close to their heels, as they scarpered into the night. I was panting, the knife still in my hand. All I could think was 'Thank God.'

I knew now that we'd been found again there was no chance they wouldn't be back, and next time they'd also come prepared to deal with Hobo. The severity of these incidents was escalating sharply. I shuddered to think what the men on the roof had been planning to do if they'd got into our flat. I felt utterly invaded and alone. It was pure luck that had saved us this time, and it seemed that there was now no place to hide. Moving house to keep safe hadn't worked. We'd covered quite a distance in our two moves already. If they had found us despite that, now it was time to leave the country.

When Max returned home from work the next morning I told him what had happened. 'It's the last straw,' I said.

It was very clear that the underground movement were hell bent on getting their revenge and there would be no let up. I had to do what was safest for my children. 'I'm going to get out of South Africa and start again,' I told him.

Max was downcast at my revelation.

'If you go … what about me?' His voice trailed. 'Can't we just find somewhere else here?'

I knew he liked the comfort of me running the house and taking charge of all the arrangements. He was so comfortable he was ignoring the obvious dangers of our situation. I was determined though.

'I have to leave,' I said decisively. 'It is entirely up to you what you want to do but I am leaving.'

Then Max shocked me with what appeared to be a casual suggestion. 'Look,' he said, 'don't you think we should team up more?'

'What do you mean?'

'Well, you know. Get married,' he said.

My first reaction was 'Absolutely not'. My first marriage had been such a disaster that I didn't ever want to go there again. Besides, although proceedings were well under way I still wasn't officially divorced from Roger.

'I'm sorry, Max,' I said, 'I am not looking for romance. I think we're better off as we are.'

'But we do everything together anyway,' he said sulkily.

I didn't reply but it surprised me that he thought that. Max didn't take on any responsibility. That wasn't doing things 'together' in my book.

In the days after he first made the offer, I found myself wondering what he imagined being married might be like. He was a nice guy but he definitely wasn't for me. He didn't inspire me with his partnership skills. He basically just wanted someone to look after him and I already had two kids to do that for.

I began searching the papers for employment abroad and discovered that accounting skills were needed in Rhodesia and New Zealand. Rhodesia was too close to South Africa for my comfort so I started pursuing opportunities in New

Zealand. After a few days, Max decided he didn't want to stay in South Africa alone and asked if he could join us. He said he would also write off for jobs as between us we'd have a better chance.

'OK,' I said doubtfully. 'Give it a go.'

Unfortunately, a single mother with two children was not an attractive prospect in New Zealand and I received floods of rejection letters. There seemed no hope of a visa. A couple of weeks after he started trying, however, Max received a letter from a bakery in Wellington. He grinned as he held it out for me to read.

*Dear Mr. Wallace,*
*We are happy to offer you the position of maintenance*
*engineer at our factory. There is an allowance for travel*
*expenses and a house to accommodate your family near our*
*plant. The offer is conditional upon the production of suitable*
*references and a marriage certificate, which we will be happy*
*to receive at your convenience.*

This offer was clearly for a married man. Max waved the letter at me. 'Judy,' he said, 'will you marry me now? If you do we can take this offer of a job and a house. We'd all be safe in New Zealand, and if it didn't work out we could go our separate ways. At least we'd be out of South Africa. What do you say?'

I knew it was vital for us to leave and it seemed there was no way I could get work on my own. I needed the children to be safe and here was an opportunity for the taking. Although I had no romantic feelings towards Max, we got on as friends and he seemed to enjoy having the kids around. I sometimes watched him playing games with them outside, just messing around, and it was as if he was a kid himself. I was faced with a dilemma. If I didn't marry Max would I jeopardize the chance for us all to be free from fear?

'I do understand your concerns and reservations,' he said, 'but I would never hurt you or the children, Judy. You know that.'

It crossed my mind that the emotional scars from my relationship with Roger might stop me from trusting a man ever again. Max was gentle and loyal yet here I was, turning him down because he didn't have the perfect partnership skills. Maybe I was being too picky? After all, he was prepared to move halfway around the world to be with me. I really had to think about this.

'Can I sleep on it?' I asked.

'Of course!' Max was beaming. As far as he was concerned this was a step up. When he had proposed before he'd been met with a flat refusal.

The next morning two more rejection letters addressed to me came in the post. I ate my toast slowly and watched Jude and David through the kitchen window as they messed around with Hobo in the sunshine. I wanted to protect them more than anything in the whole world. I brewed some coffee and then saw Max arriving from the night shift, smiling at the kids and walking up to the apartment. I poured him a coffee before he even entered the front door.

'Thanks,' he said, taking it from me and sitting at the table. 'Any toast?'

'Yes,' I said without moving, looking him in the eye.

He looked at me tentatively. 'Are you saying yes to what I think you're saying yes too?'

I nodded. 'We'll give it our best shot,' I said.

'Here's to our new life,' he beamed as he raised his coffee cup.

He stood up and kissed me on the lips very softly. My heart didn't flutter though I kissed him back. I had no idea what I was letting myself in for.

# Chapter Eighteen

$I$ was certainly streetwise when I met Max, but years of being forced to suppress my feelings had taken a serious toll on my emotional development. I had never known love or care from any man and my understanding of what a loving relationship should be simply didn't exist. I was twenty-six, but still knew nothing about the rituals of attraction. I believed that I was there to serve, that husbands had rights to take from their wives. Intimacy and love were not connected, to me. That I might have been a person with equal needs never entered my head.

When our circumstances changed and Max got offered the job, something shifted inside me. We had our 'get out' clause and an agreement that if things didn't work out we could go our separate ways, but he had found a solution to our problems and somewhere deep within me I felt beholden. When he asked me to share his bed, I mutely agreed.

Max accepted the job and explained that we planned to marry once we had arrived in New Zealand. Much to my relief this was accepted by the company, and the travel arrangements were put into place – they would send the tickets when it was all organized. I called my divorce lawyer and asked him to hurry up the proceedings, which seemed to be dragging on for ever. In fact, the final papers only arrived on 7th November, 1973, once we were in New Zealand.

Living at Knights Park while not yet having a date of departure was very stressful. Every day I waited for the postman hoping against hope that our tickets would arrive. Max was still working the night shift and sitting alone in the flat, the awful presence of the men on the roof clung to every surface, sending adrenaline pumping through my veins. I couldn't wait to leave and get my family out of there, especially once I discovered that I was pregnant with Max's baby.

Max was thrilled to bits that he was going to have a child of his own. 'I'm going to be a real Dad,' he said proudly.

Although I was pleased to be having another baby I was very aware that this situation brought a new dimension to our relationship. It wasn't just going to be a 'marriage of convenience' now. Max was the baby's dad and we were a family. Creating a strong family foundation had always been my priority. And these responsibilities were even greater now that a new baby was on the way.

After what seemed an eternity we finally received our travel documents. We packed our cases, and I arranged for a kind neighbour to take Hobo, much to the kids distress. As we left Knights Park relief flooded me. We were embarking on a new life and I felt a great sense of hope for the future. The three-week journey across the ocean was just what we needed to forget the awful stress of the past few months and give us the strength to face the new challenges ahead. I was now almost four months pregnant. Our baby would be born in this new land of opportunity.

Once in New Zealand we caught the train to Wellington. The countryside was beautiful, with ribbon-like rivers weaving in between vibrant green hills dotted with grazing sheep. Our house was in the suburbs, not far from Max's job. As we opened the door the kids burst in with excitement and ran around. Immediately it felt like home. I enrolled Jude and David in the local school and Max got down to work.

Over the next couple of months we enjoyed decorating the house and buying things for our new arrival. The birth, when it came, was easier than anticipated and after a few hours of labour our baby daughter was born.

Max was utterly charmed by her and Jude and David squealed with excitement over her little fingers and soft baby hair. We decided to call her Carolyn.

'Carrie,' David christened her. 'Baby Carrie.'

A couple of weeks after the birth Max and I got married in the registry office in Wellington. Carrie slept through the service and then we took the children for a meal afterwards. It was a strange day. I felt no emotion – no celebration, no bonding. It was very surreal, as though it was happening to someone else.

Six months after Carrie's birth, Max came home from work looking downcast. He slumped in a chair in the living room.

'Whatever's the matter?'

'Lost my job.'

'What happened?'

He murmured something non-committal and I couldn't get a straight answer out of him. 'I'll look for something else,' he mumbled.

I was dreadfully worried and suddenly felt very insecure. Our house went with the job that Max had just lost. Homelessness to me was a deep-rooted nightmare. Not a day went by when I didn't remember the feeling of being desperate on the streets by myself as a child. Now I was frantic with worry about what I would do if that happened with my lovely children in tow.

There was a shortage of property to rent in New Zealand at that time and it quickly became clear that finding a new home was not going to be easy. I wrote dozens of letters on Max's behalf and managed to get him a job in Auckland, but there was no accommodation with the job and the pay wasn't good. Every day I combed the local papers for a flat to rent and left my details anywhere I could think of that might help. During every journey I made, I was desperately looking for a garage or a shed that could provide some kind of shelter if the worst came to the worst. After a few weeks of looking I was in a state of panic. The money had all but run out.

Then one day, at end of my tether, I had a familiar symptom: I was sick straight after breakfast. I saw the children off to school and sat with Carolyn in my arms. 'Another baby on the way, sweetie pie,' I murmured. It was July 1974.

Finally, that afternoon, I found an unusual solution to our problem. I had scanned the papers for housing as usual. There was nothing suitable so I leafed through the rest of the small ads. A couple of pages in, there was a boxed advertisement: 'Bus for sale – $1,000'. I was immediately taken back to Belle Vue and those happy times I spent touring with Speedy in his bus.

We didn't even have a thousand cents to spare, never mind a thousand dollars, but I decided to give it a go. I rang the number and a cheery voice answered the phone. I arranged to go for a viewing.

Alistair and Georgia were leaving Auckland and selling everything they couldn't take with them. The bus was an old-fashioned single decker with all the seats taken out to make an empty shell inside. We took it for a test drive and the engine sounded in good shape, the tyres were new and I could see that the interior was big enough to house us all comfortably.

'I really do want to buy the bus, but I can't pay for it all at once,' I said to him. 'I can give you the money in instalments though. Would that be alright?'

'Instalments would be fine,' he said, and we shook hands on the deal.

There was a campsite near Max's work where we could stay reasonably cheaply, and they would provide electricity and toilet facilities. Max was delighted that I had solved the problem, but our relationship by this stage was becoming very strained. I had often wondered what it was that shaped our paths in life – those who travel easily, those who ride on the backs of others, or those who are left abandoned. Now, I felt that Max was riding on my back and he was a heavy weight. I worried that if I didn't keep upright and strong we would all fall over. This was not a good time to be expecting a fourth child.

Setting up the bus was hard work. We divided the area inside into two, and Max helped to put up a dividing wall.

The back end became a bedroom for the children, complete with bunks for Jude and David and a cot for Carrie. In the other half we created a small kitchenette and fitted a fold-down sofa then I bought some wood and the kids helped me to build a bolt-down table with two benches on either side. I altered some old gingham tablecloths into curtains and cushion covers. By the end the place was warm and cosy and it was all ours.

However, we had only been living there for a couple of months when Max walked out of his job. He wouldn't explain himself properly to me, saying only that he didn't like the people he worked with and didn't see why he should stay. The fact that we relied on his wage didn't seem to have entered his head.

'I'll set up on my own,' he said. 'There are loads of businesses that need an engineer and I'll get plenty of work – probably more than I do at the moment.'

I couldn't believe how naïve he was. 'Max, you need money to start up your own business, to buy equipment and advertise yourself. How are you going to do all that?'

Max was at his most maddening during these conversations, convinced that his pie-in-the-sky idea would somehow just happen. I tried to help by going round all the local restaurants and shops, cafés and hairdressers, anywhere I could think of, asking if they needed Max's expertise, but it was doomed from the start because Max had no organizational skills whatsoever, and being pregnant and looking after three small children, I couldn't help more than I already was.

I decided that we should use the bus to go in search of freelance work for Max. During the next few months we spent a week here, two weeks there, travelling to wherever there might be any kind of work and making the most of what each area could offer the children. I was keen for them to get out and experience the world and tried to make our travels educational for them. I taught them to read maps and timetables and made up algebra questions about the amount of petrol we'd used against the mileage we'd done. We'd have nature studies by a wood and learn about the different trees, birds and animals, finding out which berries and mushrooms were edible. One of the children's favourite games was paddling in a stream looking for sparkling rocks with minerals in them and learning about the gold rush. Basically, I wanted to pass on to my kids the survival skills that I had learned on the street, but to do so in a way that was safe and fun, with me behind them at all times.

There were some happy times, but by late October 1974 I'd reached the point of no return. We had no money. Max was hopeless, and I was spending more time looking for work than he spent actually doing it.

One night I sat down and told him straight. 'Max, I want to go back to Wellington. I need to have my baby in the same place that Carrie was born, somewhere that people know me and where I feel safe.'

He agreed straightaway.

When we arrived in Wellington, Max got a job almost at once but it was hardly any time before he was sacked again. He was characteristically vague about what had gone on but this time I made my own enquiries and discovered he had blown up some machinery at the factory. There was worse to come. The factory had reported Max to the authorities and they discovered he had never actually passed any professional exams. Max should not have been

allowed to work as an engineer in New Zealand – or anywhere. The only way he could do so was to pass the country's compulsory exams. I was horrified. When I'd first met
Max in South Africa, he'd told me that he was qualified and
I'd had no reason to doubt him. In fact, it turned out he'd
been working for years under totally false pretences.

Our future was on the line again, but this time things
were as bad as they could get. I feared our home would be
lost, for without a salary how would I ever be able to pay
the instalments for the bus? There was high unemployment
in New Zealand in the 1970s and the country did not need
an immigrant without skills joining the queue for a job.

Max had to take casual work – anything that would put
some cash in his hand, and provide us with some kind of
living. He took no part in any of our practical arrangements and I began to realize more and more that he lived in
a dream world, and that his idea of family life was to be tak-
en care of like one of the children. His behaviour was certainly akin to theirs in many respects and I was more of a
mother figure to him than a partner. For me this was
almost unbearably frustrating and stressful. I felt snowed
under with all the responsibilities on my plate.

In January he had to attend college every day for a few
hours to study for his licence. Then, to make ends meet, he
had to do casual work at a meat-packing factory, working
shifts. This had a devastating effect on his personality. He
couldn't cope, and sank into deep depression and apathy.
This schedule was only ever going to be short term, but he
couldn't seem to see anything beyond the immediate.

Meanwhile, the date of the exams was looming. Max was
very nervous. He was not a studious person and found the
eight-week course difficult. I tried to help by going through

the questions with him, but it was hard work and the pressure was really on. In just two months time our baby would be born and if he failed the exams he couldn't stay and work in New Zealand.

The day came and we all wished him luck. I hoped against hope that he would do well. Everything depended on it.

'How did it go?' I asked him when he came home.

'Dunno,' he said shrugging his shoulders.

He wouldn't meet my eyes, and soon turned round and left the bus. He didn't return home till late that night and, as he crawled into bed, I could tell he'd had a lot to drink.

My worst fears were realized a week or so later when an envelope containing two letters arrived. One told Max personally that he had disastrously failed the exams and would not be receiving a licence. The other was a copy that had been sent to the Department of Labour giving a full report and stating categorically: 'This man should never be employed as a maintenance engineer as his work is assessed as positively dangerous.'

My stomach and throat constricted and I felt as though I were being sucked into a deep black hole. I couldn't tell which was pounding more – my heart or my head.

'Oh Max,' was all I could say as I sank to the sofa.

I looked up at him and saw that he was close to tears. This was it – he would not now be able to get a proper job in New Zealand.

Once my head had cleared and I could view the options and obstacles that lay ahead I sat down with Max to discuss our next move. We realized there was no alternative. We had to leave the country. But where would we go? South Africa was out of the question and the only place we knew that we could get help while Max was on the dole was back in England. So that's what we decided.

I placed an ad offering the bus for sale with a heavy heart, but before I could think any further than that, I was admitted to hospital with high blood pressure. Lying in bed, I was anxious about leaving Max to cope with everything when I was away. He could hardly cope with himself never mind the kids as well. There was nothing for it, though. I was heavily pregnant and under doctor's orders.

I went into labour on the morning of April 17th and it wasn't long before I realized that this baby, like her siblings, was going to make a speedy appearance.

'I do have very quick births,' I warned the nurse.

She examined me quickly. 'The baby's not ready yet, dear. I'll come back and see you in a little while.'

Soon after she left the room, I felt the baby starting to come. I rang the bell frantically but nobody responded. I rang it again and again, and still there was no one. I held on for as long as I could but my baby was very determined. I was alone in the room so the only choice I had was to deliver the little one myself. My beautiful baby girl made her dramatic entrance in seconds and I gathered her to me as best I could. She briefly opened her big blue eyes as if to say 'hello' and then let out a strong healthy cry. This at last brought the sound of rushing feet along the corridor.

'Oh my goodness,' said the startled nurse. 'You weren't kidding, were you?'

I couldn't wait for visiting time so I could see my other children and check that everything was all right at home. The older kids were very self-sufficient, but Carrie was just a toddler and needed a great deal of care and attention. I had to put my faith in Max's abilities, but I couldn't help having concerns.

'Don't worry Mum,' Jude said forthrightly. 'We've got it all sorted.'

I took her at her word and relaxed a little. It was some time later when I discovered the truth – that Max hadn't coped at all. He'd asked a friend of mine to look after Carrie until the older ones got home from school, then it was Jude and David who took the full responsibility. They bathed and fed their sister, changed nappies and played with her until bedtime. I was so proud of them. They saw what needed to be done and got on with it without question. But I was utterly furious with Max. Two children aged nine and ten had managed to keep the boat afloat where he had completely failed.

Shortly after the baby – who we called Erin – and I got home, I found some buyers for the bus. We agreed a price of three thousand dollars, a profit of two thousand more than I had originally paid for it, which gave me enough money to buy tickets back to the UK.

By now the awful strain of the past few months was catching up with me and between that and having a new baby, I was exhausted. I badly needed to find some kind of secure home for us and take some time off from worrying for a while.

# Chapter Nineteen

The day we left, the kids and I stood on deck and watched the coastline of New Zealand disappear. It was a sad moment. I'd had so many hopes for the future when we'd arrived there two years before.

When we got to England we travelled to Weston-Super-Mare because I'd managed to book us a holiday flat there through a property magazine called *Dalton's Weekly*. I hoped it would tide us over until Max got a job. He immediately signed on the dole, but the labour exchange wasted no time and found him an unskilled position as a packer at a bakery in Bristol. With that huge hurdle scaled, somewhere permanent to live was next on the list.

After days of trudging the streets and visiting estate agents, I realized that we had come back to Britain just as the private rental market was at its lowest ebb and reaching crisis point. There were very few houses available, and with my low budget and large family I had no chance at all. Everyone was very apologetic and wished me luck, but all I could think was, 'Here we go again.'

Then one day I came across an article about some new flats being built by a private company and going for rent in

Portishead, a small town not far from Bristol. The flats were advertized as 'small with two bedrooms' and were for families with two children only. The rent was reasonable and the company offered the security of annual leases. We were getting desperate. The end of our let at the holiday flat was approaching fast and the options were limited.

'Do what you think is best,' was Max's only comment.

I went to the estate agents' office and told a lie. When they asked how many children I had, I said 'two'. I didn't go to view the flats, just signed the application form and handed it over there and then, and our application was successful.

We were lucky to be given a place on the ground floor. I explained to the kids that there was an old lady upstairs (which was true) and that they would need to be quiet when playing indoors. I figured that if people didn't hear them much they wouldn't guess how many kids there were. Within weeks the older kids started at their new schools. Max was back working shifts and as we needed the money I found a part-time job waitressing at a local coffee shop in the mornings. It was a relief to be bringing in some badly needed extra cash.

I asked Max if he could look after the two little ones from when his night shift ended until I got back from my job at one o'clock in the afternoon. His face told a story as he replied, 'What am I supposed to do with them all that time?'

One day I came home to find Carrie and Erin on the floor crying hysterically and Max snoring his head off in the bedroom. I was so angry I swiped the pillow from under his head and bellowed 'When are you ever going to grow up?'

'I hate it here,' he sniped back. 'I hate it.'

From the day we arrived in the UK Max had shrouded himself in a cloak of misery. He hated everything. He didn't like his job, he hated having to catch the bus to work, the flat was tiny and the weather was rubbish. He found fault everywhere he looked. Now I could no longer trust him with the children, I had to give up my job, which meant that we had even less money.

A couple of weeks after that, Max came home, sat down beside me and took my hand. We had been squabbling every day. I was infuriated by his refusal to take responsibility. Now he had clearly been thinking about what I said.

'You're right,' he admitted. 'I need to be a proper dad and husband. I need to stand on my own two feet. But I can't bear it here, Judy. I hate this country. There's a job going in South Africa. I want to go back there.'

It took a little while for this to sink in but Max kept talking. He promised he was going to do something worthwhile for me and the kids.

'You'll see,' he said. 'I'll prove it to you. I'll have a job and I'll get a house. I promise I'll send money when I get my first pay cheque. Will you come out when I have it all ready?'

I didn't mind him leaving. We'd been living separate lives since long before Erin was born and I simply didn't trust him any more. 'Maybe this is a chance for you to grow up and take charge of your life, but your actions will have to speak much louder than words before I can believe any of your promises,' I told him.

It was then Max told me he'd used the whole of that month's salary to buy his plane ticket. I went white. I couldn't believe it. It was our only source of income.

\* \* \*

Max left towards the end of 1976. We said our goodbyes and as he walked through the front door I felt a twinge of sadness. He'd been in our family for almost six years and yet he'd hardly impacted on the children's lives at all. His only contribution had been financial – and that had been erratic. For myself I couldn't help feeling an overwhelming sense of relief and liberation. He'd been a heavy millstone round my neck.

However, with Max gone I was left with no money and had to rely solely on our family allowance, which was supposed to supplement the family's income not be the only source. I couldn't go to the council and ask them to house me because I had a husband who should have been supporting me and in those days that meant you weren't entitled to benefits. I was deeply worried because even though I was an expert at stretching every penny, I knew the family allowance simply wasn't enough to feed myself and four children, never mind paying to keep our tiny flat warm.

I didn't want the kids to realize how worried I was about finding enough food so I made a game out of the daily struggle to put dinner on the table. They had grown up on what we called 'nothing dinners'. I prided myself that I could make five bob's worth of vegetables last for days. I started by making a soup then, as that dwindled, I added lentils or barley and finally baked whatever was left into a pie. I never threw anything away – I couldn't afford to.

'What would you like to eat today, kids?' I'd say.

'Nothing dinner!' they shouted in unison.

They had no idea.

As the weeks passed and there was still no cheque from Max in the post as he'd promised, our situation became even more difficult. I scoured the shops for bargains, buying bashed tins with no labels for pennies. This was something else I made a game of. At dinner time, each child had to pick a tin and we opened them with great excitement. The rules were that whatever was inside had to be served on the same plate and then eaten. Nothing could be wasted. The kids named their dish, and we all took a vote on which one was the best. We had some very adventurous dinners. Mushy peas, peaches and tuna was a big hit, as was hot dogs, pilchards and sponge pudding. It crossed my mind that one day a tin of dog food would end up on the plates. That would have been a step too far, even for me.

I was always planning our next meal and lay awake at night, haunted by the hungry memories of my own childhood. Would I end up foraging in the rubbish bins to feed the children? How bad would things get? I dreaded the day when I couldn't manage and my kids would go to bed hungry.

On one occasion there was nothing left in the house and it was another two days until the child allowance would be paid. I racked my brains and eventually, in desperation, came up with an idea. I sometimes bought food at a street market a couple of miles away and on a couple of occasions I had accidentally left packages behind that I had paid for. Now I set off, on foot, back to the stall in question.

'I'm sorry,' I said, 'I think left a bag of sprouts here. Did you find them?'

The stallholder smiled. 'Sure, love,' he said. 'People are always leaving things behind.'

He weighed out a large brown paper bag of sprouts and handed them over. For two days we had sprout and onion patties.

'Special burgers,' I told the kids.

I don't know what I would have done if my ploy hadn't worked.

One day as the kids and I were cleaning up the garden area round our flat the caretaker of the building came up.

'Excuse me, love,' he said, 'but how many children have you got living here?'

I realized there was no point lying again. 'Four,' I said.

'I thought so, but listen I'm not going to tell anyone. Had I not seen you all together I'd never have known. Your kids are well behaved and very quiet. Just be careful,' he advised.

That brief warning niggled, but with the Christmas holidays looming I put it to the back of my mind while other worries took over. I'd still had no word or money from Max and it had been ten or eleven weeks. Things were very tight.

We set about decorating the house ready to welcome the festive season. David made a Christmas tree out of a box from the local supermarket; Jude cut up and painted newspapers to make paper chains; Carrie stuck pictures on some empty toilet rolls and Erin filled them with dolly mixtures to make crackers.

I asked the butcher for some bones, thinking I could make a tasty stew out of them for Christmas dinner but I think he felt sorry for us because he came back with two bags, one of bones and the other wrapping a huge piece of belly pork. 'Four pence will do,' he said kindly. 'Happy Christmas.'

'Thank you so much,' I said, overwhelmed with gratitude.

The man just nodded and smiled. After weeks of eking meals out of vegetables and barley, this was an amazing feast.

Then on Christmas Eve we had another wonderful surprise. There was a loud knock on the door. I was busy with the baby so David went to answer it. There was nobody there. He looked down and saw that a hamper had been left on our step and, ever resourceful, he dragged it in shouting 'Hey, everyone, look what I found.'

We all gathered round. A card was tied to the handle of the hamper, which read 'From the Rotary Club, Portishead – Merry Christmas.' We lifted the lid and the kids sat wide-eyed and open-mouthed as we took out the contents. We had never had such treats in our lives. There was a Christmas cake, cheese, chicken, ham, chocolates, crackers – it was untold treasure. I was so touched I couldn't speak. During my life, only a handful of people had ever been spontaneously generous to me without expecting something in return and it always made me feel very emotional.

This act of kindness was for us all the true meaning of Christmas. I never did find out for sure who told the Rotary Club that I was on my own with the kids and scraping for every penny but I suspect it might have been the caretaker. Whatever the case, it was our best Christmas ever.

# Chapter Twenty

New Year 1977 brought very little peace of mind for me. There was still no word from Max, and I was beginning to panic that he had buzzed off and left us destitute. It was a cold winter and the children needed clothes and school uniforms and the bills were piling up. Then to top it all, a letter arrived from the housing association stating that someone had reported us for having too many children in the flat. An agent was coming to see me and would file a report.

I immediately went to see the caretaker. He was visibly upset and assured me that he had no idea who the whistle-blower might have been. He promised to put in a good word for me.

Then, in March, six months after he'd left for South Africa, I finally received a letter from Max. He enclosed a cheque, and after the months of hard struggle I could at last straighten out the unpaid bills. His letter was full of enthusiasm. His friend John had got him the job at a bakery but this time he was a foreman and head of stores. He said the job was well paid and that he had found a nice house to rent.

'It's perfect,' he wrote. 'You will love it. I am so lonely and miss you and the children. Please, please give me another chance. I want to look after you and the kids. I miss you, Judy. Please think about coming over.'

Max's enthusiasm did not rub off on me. He had taken six months to write and tell me this news and my situation had been dire all the time I was waiting. Now he thought he could make everything all right with a promise or two. I was far too familiar with his idealistic dreams. Life with him had been nothing but stress. Things had been very tough, but I had been happier finding solutions on my own. I just needed a bit more time to figure out how I was going to manage by myself long term.

The interview with the landlord's agent did not go well. The rules of the lease were clear and I had broken them. He said I could stay in the flat until the end of my current lease but the company would not renew it after that. I had just over three months to find somewhere else to live. I was beside myself as the spectre of homelessness once again reared its head. This time I had absolutely no income to play with and I knew how cutthroat the rental market was.

Early one morning, before the kids went to school, the postman delivered another letter from Max, and just as I went to pick it up the caretaker knocked on my door. I could tell by his face that he really didn't want to be there.

'I'm sorry, love,' he began apologetically, 'but I've received a letter from the office giving me instructions.' He cleared his throat awkwardly. 'It says here that when you leave, you have to give your keys to me.'

'But I don't have to get out for a couple of months yet.'

'I know, love, I think it's their way of reminding you.' He nodded his head then lifted his hand in a little 'sorry' gesture. As I closed the door I put my back against it and closed my eyes.

When I opened Max's letter I saw that this time he had included a hand-drawn picture of the house he had rented. It looked big with large bay windows and a huge garden.

'I'm sure there won't be any trouble like before,' he wrote. 'It's been a long while since you were here – no one will remember Jude's case.'

It was nice to realize that he was thinking about what was important to me. Then he went on: 'Because I still have my residence permit and we're married and I'm fully employed here, you and the kids are allowed to come and join me. The South African Embassy will pay your fares. Please come, Judy.'

I sat with Max's letter in my hand and the caretaker's words in my ear. Did I have the right to keep Carrie and Erin away from their father if there was a chance for them to form a relationship with him? This question and many more whirled round and round in my mind. Would it be better for us to function as a family once more? I was torn and confused.

At dinner that night I discussed everything with Jude and David. Jude was nearly twelve and David eleven so they were old enough to understand what was going on. I explained that we had to leave the flat and told them about the opportunity we had to return to South Africa where Max had rented a big house with a garden.

'I think that Max is working hard to make amends. Do you two want to think about it?' I asked.

Both Jude and David didn't like Portishead and the prospect of a more comfortable home and life in the sunshine appealed to them. Their eyes lit up and I knew that the decision had been made. The truth was that it seemed the best option.

We sailed to Cape Town and when we arrived, Max was standing on the dock holding a huge bunch of flowers. He flung his arms round me and cuddled the kids, obviously delighted to see us. 'I'm so glad you've come,' he kept repeating.

It was such a different welcome from the one I'd received when I'd returned to Roger in Lebanon that I couldn't help feeling a little flicker of optimism.

We caught a train to Johannesburg and then took a taxi from the station.

'Where's the new house?' asked David.

'How big is it?' Jude questioned. 'Will I have my own bedroom?'

They were firing questions at Max in their excitement. A place with a garden – how fantastic was that? Max had painted such a rosy picture and none of us could wait to see it.

'Won't be too long now,' the taxi driver told us. After a few more minutes he announced, 'Almost there. 10 Bealearts Street, Troyville.'

Troyville, I thought? He must be joking. I'd been writing to him care of the bakery's post office box, so I had no idea that the house he'd found was in such a notoriously derelict area. Reality soon set in when he parked outside a very run-down property. It bore a faint resemblance to Max's drawing but certainly not to the picture he'd painted in his letters. It had obviously been a grand house once, in colonial times, but years of neglect had left it flaking and crumbling. Troyville had been abandoned by its residents years ago, and with boarded-up shops and empty factories it was now a haven for the homeless and unemployed. Drunken tramps mindlessly threw their empty cans and bottles into overgrown gardens from streets that stank of urine. The garden we'd all been dreaming of was littered with debris. I couldn't believe my eyes. We had travelled thousands of miles to live in a derelict slum.

Maybe it'll be better inside, I thought, hanging on to one last shred of hope. The kids ran ahead in excitement, but it wasn't long before they met us on the veranda with puzzled faces.

'It's got no furniture, Mum,' cried Jude.

'It's empty,' added David.

Max didn't say anything so I went to look for myself. The house was huge with long corridors and large bedrooms. The whole place was decaying inside and needed a complete overhaul to be safely habitable. There were thick layers of dust everywhere. In each bedroom there was a bed. Nothing else.

I was speechless.

'Max, what . . ?' I questioned.

'I got it 'cos it's near to work,' he said.

He then told me that he had used his salary for that month to buy the beds.

'Oh no, not again,' I thought. 'What are we going to buy food with?' I asked him.

'I can bring bread and stuff from the bakery.'

I took a very deep breath and tried to control my shock. It was a massive let-down, but this was the way it was and though my heart sank at the prospect, we had to make the best of it.

Max borrowed some money to buy a three-piece suite from a second-hand shop, so that we at least had something to sit on. The kids and I tried to scrub the place clean, but no matter how you looked at it the house was still a dump.

It wasn't long before things fell into the same old patterns. Max took on extra shifts at work and was hardly at home, leaving me to struggle with the children, scraping to put enough food on the table. Then one day a few months on I went into the kitchen to find Carrie standing rooted to the spot in shock.

'Whatever's the matter, baby,' I asked, picking her up. She pointed at the window terrified. There was a dead rat hanging from a piece of string that had been tied to the window lock. I couldn't imagine who would have put it there, but there were always tramps hanging around so it was probably one of them. I cut the poor creature down and threw it in the bin.

Alone in bed that night the memory of the rat made my blood boil. I was acutely aware that it was only too easy to get into the house and that any one of the drunken vagrants who hung around outside could do so at will. I locked all the doors but every tiny sound echoed through the empty rooms.

When Max finally came home and I told him about Carrie and the rat, he shrugged his shoulders and showed no concern. I knew I was fighting a losing battle. Max hadn't come good on any of his promises and I was deeply unhappy. The kids were not thriving and I hated that we were living in such appalling conditions. I didn't care who had put it there – that rat was the final straw. I might have put up with living with rats back in the mill-house but I was not going back to that again.

All at once, that was it. It was definitely over.

# Chapter Twenty-one

*M*ax wanted to stay in South Africa, which was fine by me, and it was agreed that I would return to England with the children. I started making plans at once but before we left I felt that the children deserved a holiday. They had suffered a lot over the past year, what with all the moving and scraping a living from so little, and I wanted them to have an experience that would allow them to remember South Africa in a positive way. Besides, I didn't want to simply turn round and leave again, as if the whole trip had been a total waste of time. We were there, and we might as well make the most of it. Max didn't want to be involved so I asked the kids for their ideas, and Jude suggested that it would be fun to go on a bike ride.

They had been learning about the Voortrekkers (Boer pioneers) in school. In 1836 these Dutch settlers had embarked on a mass migration, abandoning their farms to escape British colonialism. They travelled from the Cape Colony into the interior of Southern Africa, a journey that became known as 'The Great Trek'. We decided that it would be fun to ride along the same route as those that trekked towards Natal. This would lead us out of the

Transvaal and through the Orange Free State, down towards Volksrust, Escort and eventually Ladysmith. Then we would travel through the Drakensburg Mountains towards our final destination. By the time we reached Durban we would have travelled 400 miles, which I estimated would take about ten days if we kept up a good pace.

Jude and David could cycle, but the little ones were too small so I had to work out a way of transporting them. I had a chat with the owner of our local bicycle store, and told him what we were planning to do. He was so amazed that he made me an offer I could not refuse.

'How would it be,' he asked, 'if we give you all the bikes free of charge, make and fit a side car, and arrange free maintenance for the duration of your journey, in exchange for some mobile advertising?'

I simply couldn't believe his generosity and found myself shaking his hand and thanking him over and over again.

Everyone we told about the ride was enthusiastic and interested and it wasn't long before the press began to ask about our plans. We flung ourselves into planning the holiday, which quickly became a full-time project.

The kids and I sat for days poring over maps and preparing our route. I explained that although this ride would be a fabulous adventure, it would not be without its frustrations and hard work and we'd all need loads of stamina. I suggested to Jude and David that they keep a daily diary, and at the end of the ride we could talk about what they had learnt from it and what it had meant to them.

We needed to toughen up before we left. Fortunately Troyville was quite a hilly area, and since the roads were pretty rough it was a good training ground for us. The side car was just the job. There were two little seats, one behind the other, for Carrie and Erin. The base of it was big enough to hold a tent and camping equipment, basic clothing and emergency repair kits. And emblazoned on the side so that nobody could miss it was the name and logo of the bicycle shop. Riding for the first time with everything in it was like driving a tank; my leg muscles were going to have an almighty workout.

At the crack of dawn on 6 November 1977, we left Johannesburg for the biggest adventure in the children's lives. At the end of that first day we arrived exhausted in the Afrikaans town of Vereeniging alongside the Vaal River. Our bikes had no gears so pedalling along some of the roads had been really tough.

Jude got off her bike, threw it to the ground and declared, 'I've had enough! I'm not going to ride another inch.'

Red in the face from heat and temper she lay for several minutes spluttering her grievances. I waited until it had all fizzled out and then said, 'OK, if you want to quit so soon, that's fine, but let's set up camp then you can decide what you want to do in the morning.'

We found a lovely spot and Jude and David went to find some water. I had brought a little blow-up plastic paddling pool. That pool turned out to be my best buy as it served so many purposes. The kids filled it with water from a standpipe they found in an abandoned garage nearby. I threw in the washing and gave them all the task of stamping on it. While this fun was going on I noticed a small bush settlement opposite. There was an old African man smoking a pipe, rocking in his chair and watching us. We continued with the washing and as the kids were hanging the clothes on the guy ropes of the tent I looked across again, and saw two Africans rocking away and watching us. By the time I had dinner cooking on the camping stove there was a whole row of them, completely engrossed. I've often wondered what they thought of that strange white family camping in the bush with inflatable pools and bicycles.

'Mum, I don't really want to quit the ride,' Jude said quietly after dinner. 'I've written it all down in my journal, but could I please write one bad word, just this once?'

Hiding a smile I told her she could and she wrote, 'Today was bloody hard.'

The next day, as we were toiling up a steep hill, we were flagged down by a passing car. The driver was a reporter for the local newspaper. Somehow he'd heard about what we were doing and decided it would make a great story. It was unheard of in South Africa at that time for a white woman to travel anywhere on a bicycle, never mind take four children from Johannesburg to Durban! So, rather hot and cross at being made to stop just when we had a good head of steam up, we agreed to pose for a photo and talk to him for a few minutes. To be honest, I didn't give it very much more thought after that.

A few days into the trip we reached a small African village near the town of Volksrust. This town's name means 'the nation rests' and it is the northern gateway to the Battlefields Route, with an impressive Majuba mountain backdrop. This is where battle-weary Boer soldiers went to recover from the rigours of war.

As we entered the village the streets were lined with people waving and cheering. I shouted to the kids to look out for whatever was happening, thinking that perhaps it was a carnival. A young African boy ran down the street waving at us to stop. 'Come, come,' he repeated.

We followed him through the crowds into the village shop where the owner ran over and embraced us. He grabbed my hand and repeated with such passion, 'You are in my shop, you are in my shop!' He then pointed to a copy of the local paper, and there on the front page was a photograph of us all. We were celebrities it seemed, and these people were all cheering for us! The owner was so delighted to have met us that he said we could choose anything we wanted from his shop to see us on our way. We were soon surrounded by villagers, who just wanted to touch us and shake our hands. As we turned our bikes round to wave goodbye they sang and stomped their feet in a farewell dance to wish us well on our journey.

The memories of that trip are still vivid in my mind. Every day brought new experiences and adventures. For example, one day we found a burnt out mission school in the bush and Jude discovered an old exercise book lying around. Inside, a young African girl had written in English, describing her life in the village. It was a fascinating insight that delighted us all.

Then there was the night of the great thunderstorm. Our tent blew down while we were sleeping and in the torrential rain I had to carry the little ones while Jude and David carried our sleeping bags to the only dry place around: an old toilet block.

After seven days we reached Estcourt, in the foothills of the Drakensburg Mountains. This was a very interesting place. Estcourt had suffered a turbulent past, from the Zulu nation's first encounter with the Boer settlers to the Anglo-Boer War. The kids' imaginations went wild as we explored the old battlefields and re-enacted some old war manoeuvres. North of the town was the site of the great siege, the place where the Boers had boxed in the main British forces. It was there that Winston Churchill had been captured as a young war correspondent. Jude and David stood on those railway tracks and were able to sense and imagine far more than any history book would ever give them.

Our biggest challenge was to travel through the Valley of a Thousand Hills. It was exhausting to get over one mountain only to be faced with yet another, and we felt as though it would never end. I was so proud of Jude and David. They gritted their teeth and pedalled as hard as they could. The highest and toughest of them all was Newcastle Hill but after what seemed an eternity we made it, and fell off our bikes absolutely shattered.

Once we'd caught our breath, we stood up and admired our prize – the view from the summit. The mountains stretched away as far as the eye could see, creating a rugged purple-hued backdrop for the tree-covered valleys below. I could feel the powerful force of nature as we stood there. It was breathtakingly beautiful. This was a view very few people would have the chance to see as it was not accessible by car; the last part of the ascent was just a track. We had the privilege of being at one with the natural world and all its beauty that day. Jude summed it up when she said, 'It's magic, just magic.'

Obviously, once you've got to the top, you get to come down again, and we lifted our feet off the pedals and sailed for miles. It was so exhilarating that the little ones in their side car kept shouting, 'Again please, again!'

Our next stop was Ladysmith, the site of another great siege between the Boers and the British. On the road to Pietermaritzburg the heavens opened and I had to place our trusty paddling pool over the heads of the little ones to keep them dry. It began to get too dangerous to ride so I started looking around for somewhere we could shelter. We were on an isolated stretch of road with only bush land surrounding us, but after a few minutes I spotted an African village ringed by fencing in the distance. This seemed to be our best option.

It was a very sodden family that headed into the village. We were greeted by an elderly African man who was absolutely amazed to see us. He took us into his hut and gave us towels to dry ourselves. No-one could speak English but the hospitality of the villagers needed no words as they brought us drinks and pieces of fruit to share. It turned out that just before our arrival the old man's granddaughter had given birth to a baby boy. She was lying on a mat cuddling him and the hut was filled with well-wishers. This was an especially moving experience for us.

I took a fifty cent coin from my pocket and placed it in the tiny hand of the newborn, as a token to bring him prosperity and luck in his life. Immediately, all the Africans in the hut fell onto their knees. They put their hands together, lifted them to their faces and bowed their heads in prayer repeating a thank you blessing in the Zulu language.

At the time, I wondered at the strength of their reaction, but I think the explanation is that there had been a severe drought for seven years in South Africa and that day, the long-prayed-for rains arrived. Zulus believe that their god is in the sun, the wind and the rain, and on the day that the rain finally came a white woman and her children had appeared out of the mist, so in their minds we were associated with it. What's more, I had blessed their child by putting money into his little fist and according to their philosophy he would now be a special child, a chosen one, whose life would be changed by these events. This was a day on which many momentous things happened. Spiritually we were all connected, despite apartheid, and I knew the villagers would be talking about us and remembering us for many years to come.

'How far have we got to go now?' asked David as he stood on a rock the next day. 'Look, I can see the sea!'

Sure enough, the beautiful coastline of Durban was visible in the distance.

'I wish I could have a swim in that water,' Jude said wistfully. The rolling surf did seem to be taunting us to jump in and bathe our hot, tired bodies. The sight of the beach spurred us on, but it was still several hours before we got there.

It was a great relief when we arrived in Durban. It had taken us eleven days, and as we rode down the main street our arrival was heralded by a huge electric storm. The thrill of achievement, as the storm boomed and crackled around us like a fanfare, was incredible. It was the first journey I had ever made that wasn't simply about survival – the first holiday I ever had – and it was great fun.

The next day we went into town and parked the bikes. When we came out of a shop a huge crowd were waiting for us with newspaper reporters and radio presenters. Somehow our story had grown and captured people's imagination. Someone must have realized we'd arrived and it seemed as though the whole town had turned out to see us. I stood proudly by as the kids gave interviews and talked to everyone with confidence. We stayed in Durban another ten days and wherever we went people waved and stopped to chat with us. It was amazing to think that so many people were inspired by what we had achieved.

When all the excitement had calmed down the children and I talked at length about the trip and all that they'd written in their diaries. They had blossomed in so many ways and I knew they would take this new-found strength with them for the rest of their lives. If you can pedal on a fixed-gear bicycle through the Valley of a Thousand Hills at the age of eleven or twelve, you can basically achieve anything!

It was a great end to a huge adventure. And now we were set to make another long journey back to the UK. I didn't know it then, but those idyllic days in Durban were one of the last carefree times we'd all share for several months to come.

# Chapter Twenty-two

The children and I got a train back to Johannesburg and went to catch our plane home at Jan Smuts Airport. Max came to see us off. He was silent as we headed for the departure gate.

'Take care,' I said, holding out my hand. I thought it would probably be the last time I'd ever see him.

He just nodded. I turned to see him walk away, with head bowed and shoulders slumped. He looked like a lost little boy.

'Stand tall, Max, for goodness sake,' I muttered as I walked on.

Before I left South Africa I was lucky enough to have found us a house to let in a little place called Byfleet, in Surrey. It wasn't very big but just the job for us to make a new start. When we got there, everything began really well. I found two cleaning jobs and the three older kids started school, while Erin attended a nursery down the road. I started to feel that I could breathe again, and for the first time in a long while I began to look to the future. We'd been back in England just a couple of months when early one evening I received a phone call from a friend of mine in Johannesburg.

'I had to call you,' she said urgently. 'It's about Max. He's in dead trouble. The police found him and John with black women in their beds.'

'You're kidding!' I yelled. It was still a criminal offence in South Africa, punishable by a prison sentence, for a white man to sleep with a black woman.

'And there's worse. There's money missing from the bakery and they don't know if it's him who has taken it.'

I was speechless. What was there left to say?

'He's done a runner,' she continued. 'I thought you should know.'

I put the phone down and sank to the sofa. 'He's only been on his own for two months,' I thought, staring at the ceiling. I was furious with Max, but also concerned. We were still married after all. Could any of this impact on me and the kids?

A week or so later there was a knock on the door. When I opened it, my heart stopped and my mouth went dry. There stood Max, suitcase and all. He looked as if he hadn't slept for weeks. His hair was greasy and he was unshaven. I was in shock.

'What the . . ?'

Before I could mutter anything else he said, 'I've nowhere to stay. Can you put me up? I never want to go back.'

I felt utterly drained and in complete turmoil.

'I want to come back and settle here.'

'Max, I know what you've done. A friend phoned and told me everything.' I was so angry I could hardly speak. 'What on earth are you thinking? You can't just turn up out of the blue and expect to be taken in. Do you really think you can just waltz in here and be rescued?'

'It wasn't me,' he said almost in tears. 'It was John, I was just there. Please, Judy, let me stay. It'll only be for a short while, maybe just a few days till I get a job. I've got no money, I'll be on the street,' he pleaded.

I felt Carrie and Erin's hands around my legs. Seeing their father on the doorstep almost in tears was not a sight I wanted them to remember.

'You'd better come in.' I said through gritted teeth.

Jude and David went to their rooms. They were as shocked as me to see their stepfather again, and not best pleased because they were old enough to be aware that he was nothing but a drain on our finances and my energy. Once the little ones were in bed I made it very clear to Max that he was on his own. He'd put me in an impossible position because of the children. I told him he could sleep on the sofa, but only as an alternative to being on the streets.

'You'd better find yourself a job quick, Max, and get yourself somewhere else to stay. This arrangement lasts as short a time as possible. Do you understand?'

It was an enormous strain for the whole family having Max in the house. Every night I prayed for news that he had got a job.

'I've got an interview next week,' he'd say. Or, 'They're going to let me know on Wednesday.'

As usual with Max, I had no idea where the lines of honesty were drawn – if they were even there at all. His flight from South Africa was clearly far more complicated and dangerous than he would ever be prepared to admit. To this day I've no idea how he managed to escape arrest.

At the beginning of the third week of Max's stay I was issued with a stinking letter and a notice of eviction. My landlord had heard that I had someone living in the house and since this was against the rules of the tenancy, I was given one month to leave. If I refused, he would take me to court.

I phoned him immediately to explain the situation, but he wasn't interested in my story. How easy it is, I thought, for backs to turn when help is needed the most. Homelessness seemed to follow me like a curse.

While I had the vital job of searching for yet another place to live, Jude or David looked after the little ones. Max's relationship with them became more and more strained. Everyone in the family had chores – even little Erin – and I had always fostered the idea that we worked together as a team. Max, however, constantly fell out of that remit and as Jude got older she resented it more and more. One day while I was out with David, Jude was doing her chores, vacuuming the carpets. The noise got on Max's nerves, and in a temper he told her to stop making such a racket.

'I am vacuuming the place,' Jude raged, 'while you sit and do absolutely nothing. You never ever do anything.'

They got into a screaming match, and when I got home the door to the lounge had a deep dent where Jude had hurled the vacuum cleaner against it.

'Whatever's been going on?' I asked her.

'It's him, Mum,' she said pointing vehemently at Max. 'He was saying horrible things in front of the little ones. He asked Carrie if she'd go with him when he left.' Jude was shaking with rage. She was very protective of her four-year-old sister.

I was livid. Throwing your own child into a state of confusion by asking them to choose between their parents was the height of wickedness in my book. I remembered too clearly the sickening feeling in my stomach when my father took me away from my sisters. He'd literally pulled me from their arms and as he dragged me down the road, a petrified little two-year-old, I could hear their screams echoing behind me. I never wanted my children to experience the sheer terror that had coursed through me that day. I marched up to Max in a fury.

'Don't you dare put a child in that position – how dare you! No-one – do you hear me – no-one splits up my children.'

He didn't say a word, just turned white and slumped on the chair.

Time was running out and I was getting desperate when I finally got lucky with my house search. I found a flat above a row of shops in Sheerwater, a huge council estate on the outskirts of Woking, Surrey. It had been empty for a long time and although it was in need of work I was glad to have it. The rent was cheap and there were schools nearby. The landlord was grateful to have someone take it over and offered me some DIY vouchers to help clean it up.

The day before we were due to leave Byfleet, Max disappeared, suitcase and all. I had told him from the beginning that he wasn't coming with us, whether he had a job or not. He must have left in the early hours. I hadn't a clue where he had gone, and I really didn't care. I gathered up the kids and locked the front door behind us. The keys went back through the letterbox and I closed the garden gate. The five of us walked slowly to the bus stop with just one suitcase between us. It felt as if life was on action replay. Here I go again, I thought, and only one suitcase to hold every single thing the five of us own.

I dug deep inside to keep my spirits up and then realized that what I needed more than anything was to draw a line under all our difficulties. There was something important I had to do first. That afternoon I made an appointment to apply for my divorce from Max.

'It'll take a few months,' I was told on the phone. 'But we can go through all that when you come in.'

I felt rejuvenated just having made the call. We might have virtually nothing, but we were on our own and could rely completely on each other. This time nothing and no-one was going to change that.

# Chapter Twenty-three

*M*oving into an empty flat with almost no possessions required all my creative skills. Just cleaning it properly took well over a week. The place was unbelievably filthy. The first time we opened the door David had tears in his eyes.

'Oh, Mum,' he said sadly as he surveyed the grime.

We scrubbed down the walls with bleach and to keep the kids' spirits up I made a game out of polishing the lino floors. I put the polish on the floor then plopped Carrie and Erin onto an old rug, dragging them backwards and forwards to rub it in.

'You're on a boat again, you're sailing the seas.'

'Faster, faster!' they both squealed.

'Hey, it's the Red Sea,' David laughed, as the colour of the lino finally appeared.

Gradually it began to look habitable.

We bought some paint and cheap wallpaper with the landlord's DIY vouchers and when we'd finished the job, it looked like a completely different flat from the first time we walked through the door. Mind you, we still had hardly any furniture and money was very tight. Luckily that first week one of the ladies I cleaned for was getting rid of her mattresses and, knowing our difficulties, she kindly handed them over. I could have kissed her. It would take several months, however, before the flat approached any condition that could have been described as 'furnished'.

Financially things were very strained. Our only income was from my two part-time cleaning jobs, which didn't amount to much, and every day the bills piled up. I worried constantly whether there would be enough money for basics like food and heating and lay awake at night working out how to spend the little money I had to the best effect.

Soon after I arrived in Sheerwater, I went to the social security office to get some help. I knew I was entitled to some financial support but when I got there at nine o'clock the place was already packed and the queues snaked back almost to the door. It was difficult to just wait when there were so many things I could have done instead, but I didn't have any options. I was due to go to work that day and hated having to ring them and say that I was tied up – I was nervous that they might fire me – but I needed this extra help. The bills were mounting and the kids were growing rapidly. Both David and Jude needed new shoes. We were completely on our own now and I was desperate for support.

The first day I waited for six hours, until I had to go and pick up Carrie and Erin from school. It was incredibly frustrating because despite the long wait I had made no progress. The next morning I returned to try again and this time I was luckier. After four or five hours I finally got to the front of the queue and explained my situation. I was painfully aware that everyone behind me could hear exactly what I was saying. It felt like washing my dirty linen in public but there was nothing for it.

'So, you've been abroad?' the lady asked me when I had finished. She made it sound as if I had been swanning around the Mediterranean on a yacht. 'We need to start your file all over again,' she snapped. 'Fill in these forms, please.'

That took hours and I had to supply birth certificates and marriage certificates as well.

'There is a backlog,' the lady said when I presented her with a huge pile of papers.

I had absolutely no money as it was and was really struggling to get food on the table every night, never mind buy clothes and pay bills. 'How long will it take?' I asked.

She hesitated. 'Oh, I don't know. Your case is complicated and it will probably take several weeks.'

My spirits sank. Even restricting myself to buying the children the few things they desperately needed second hand from the Oxfam shop I couldn't hold out for very long.

'How many weeks?' I asked, nervously.

The lady cast an eye over the paper on the very top of the pile. She had absolutely no sympathy for me and I knew I was just another case in her busy day.

'I don't know,' she said shortly. 'You'll just have to wait.'

In the end it was almost two months before I received anything. I was badly behind with the rent and the fuel bills but at least it gave me an additional £32 a week. It wasn't much but it made a huge difference and when I was offered an extra cleaning job for a couple of hours in the evening, I jumped at the chance.

Still, the kids did without a lot of things. It was difficult to see them get excited when the ice-cream van stopped in the street and then watch their disappointment when I couldn't afford four 'ninety-nines'. When Carrie's sixth birthday came around she asked if she could have a friend over.

'Like a party,' she said hopefully.

I only had a few chicken wings to make for food but I set it up like a picnic out on the balcony and they had a lot of fun, despite the meagre rations.

'Have we got a rug to sit on, Mum?' Carrie asked.

'No love,' I said, 'but if you like we can put down some newspaper and pretend.'

Most nights I made vegetables with barley and lentils and cheese. The kids never had chocolates or biscuits or even fruit. Meat was an enormous treat for them. We simply couldn't afford it.

Whenever things were really tough I encouraged them to look ahead not backwards.

'Hey guys, when we are this low down, where's the only place to go?'

'The only way is up, up, up!' they all sang.

They were very brave about it.


In spite of poverty, we still had fun and even in our most desperate times we always managed to find something to laugh at. One time I bought a cottage settee for five pounds from a charity shop. I couldn't afford the delivery charge so David, Jude and I hauled it home and manoeuvred it up the stairs ourselves. It was a heavy and difficult job and when we finally had it in place, David plopped onto the seat with a sigh. Immediately the arm pinged off and the whole thing collapsed in a heap, with poor David in the middle.

'Do you think that will happen every time?' Jude giggled.

'Give it a go,' I said.

Of course the settee collapsed again and we ended up howling with laughter at all that effort for nothing. In the end, David fixed it. At only thirteen years old, he was becoming a good little handyman. Another time I picked up a washing machine for just twelve pounds – a real bargain I thought. It worked beautifully for four days then flooded the kitchen, and the two shops downstairs as well.

'That's me back to washing clothes in the bath, then,' I said, and we flung the old machine out.

Slowly, however, despite these disasters the flat began to look like home. I might only have one pot to cook in, I thought to myself, but one pot is all I need.

I never bought a single item of clothing for myself and used to wash my clothes at night and dry them to wear the next day.

After the social security money started coming through, I managed to put a little cash aside every week by scrimping and saving until eventually there was enough money to take the children on mystery adventures. They never knew in advance where they were going. I led them onto trains or buses and they had to follow the signs along the route to try and figure out where we were heading. I took them to historic sites, castles, beaches, and all kinds of interesting places – anywhere we could reach and get back home from within a day. On the way back, to add to the fun and help the younger ones to become self-reliant, we played a game where I pretended I was deaf, blind and mute, and it was their job to lead me home. If I spoke, or helped them in any way, they lost the game.

This game required huge organizational skills and brought on noisy debates.

'No, it's this way,' one would shout. 'Look, that's platform two.' Or, 'Where's the sign? Quick we're going to miss it.' I was whipped up stairs, taken down in lifts, pulled by my arms in a rush to catch the next bus on time, and I couldn't utter a word. Only once did we get on the wrong train. I knew it, but couldn't let on. I sat hoping against hope that they would all soon realize. Then, at the last minute David shouted, 'Get her off, get her off, we're on the train to Cornwall!' I often wondered what the other passengers must have thought as my noisy entourage hastily shoved me off the train. It may sound frivolous, but I wanted all my children to learn how to get about by themselves just in case they ever needed to. I'd had no one to teach me and had learned the hard way; I was helping them to learn the fun way!

Still, I was very tired. Holding down three part-time jobs and looking after four children was a lot to take on and the constant juggling of bills took its toll. I seemed to spend all day rushing from one job to another, doing the school run or making my way to a shop or market stall where I knew I could get a bargain. No sooner had I managed to pay the gas bill than the rent was due. Every penny counted. I used to use one teabag for ages, dunking it in the water again and again to keep me going. Every little helped. There were days when all I'd have for dinner was a tiny square of cheese and some barley. It was better than nothing. I suppose I must have a very strong constitution to survive all the physical hardship I've lived through. I'm grateful for that because if I'd got ill and couldn't work, we'd all have been sunk.

\* \* \*

When we'd been in Sheerwater a few months, I got a letter from my sister Mary one day. She said she was writing to let me know that Dad had died in South Africa and he was leaving all his money to Cherie, his girlfriend after Freda. I felt as though I was hearing about some distant neighbour rather than my own flesh and blood. I didn't feel relief or anger or anything. I put the letter away and carried on with my day, barely giving it a second thought. Later in life, when I looked back, I felt angry that he had got off scot free; he'd caused so much damage and been allowed to get away with it all. However, that day my main reaction was indifference.

A few months later my past came back to haunt me again when there was a knock at the door one evening. I had finished work for the day and was helping the kids with their homework.

'I'll get it,' David jumped up. A second later he came back. 'Mum, there's a couple of old ladies at the door,' he whispered.

I made my way to the open door. It took a second before I recognized them. 'Oh my goodness,' I thought, 'what on earth are they doing here?'

'Mum?' I said, incredulous, and then, to my older sister, 'Dora?'

'Can I come in?' my mother asked, 'I need your help.'

I couldn't believe it. I'd written to give her my new address after we moved there but after all this time and having let me down so often, what on earth was she doing on my doorstep?

# Chapter Twenty-four

The kids were flabbergasted. David and Jude, who were older and had more understanding of the situation, were not very interested and quickly went off to their bedrooms. It was time for Carrie and Erin to go to bed in any case and I packed them off after a few introductions.

'What's wrong?' I asked my mother, when I got back.

Mum had aged. She looked very weary. Dora sat on a chair sucking her teeth, then clicking them together to make as much noise as she could. She looked absolutely terrible. She was still only forty but her hair was white and matted together in spiky clumps, and her cheeks were puffy. Back in the old days she had been a model and worked in the movies, so I was shocked to see how much she had changed. She had never been friendly towards me after Dad snatched me from home. The few times I visited as a child she hadn't wanted to play with me and later, when I came back from South Africa, she had left me at the train station on my own, despite promising to pick me up and take me to our mother's house.

'I'm at my wits end,' Mum explained. 'I didn't know where to go or what to do. It's Dora. She's been really ill. In and out of hospital. I can't cope, Judy.'

I could hardly believe what I was hearing. I was sure that things must be bad for Mum to take the trouble to find me but the sheer brass neck of her visit was a shock. I hadn't seen her since the day she had refused even to catch my eye while Roger attacked me in her kitchen.

'I need help,' she said. 'It's as simple as that.'

I knew what it was like to have a back turned on me in times of trouble and I always swore that I'd do my best to help anyone I could. Now here was my own mother asking for my assistance.

'I'll put the kettle on,' I offered. 'Let's see what we can do.'

Mum poured out the whole story. Dora had been very ill and was a difficult patient. She often phoned the police for no reason and had all kinds of problems, accusing her doctor of unprofessional conduct and getting into arguments with the neighbours. No one wanted to deal with her and one by one the family had abandoned ship until even Dora's own son, who was in his early twenties, refused to take any responsibility. Dora had escaped from the hospital where she had been placed and was now living near my mother, who had tried everything she could think of to help.

'I don't know what to do,' Mum sighed.

I weighed things up. The summer holidays were just about to start and perhaps it would be a good idea to take the younger kids to their grandmother's house in Wales for a couple of weeks. After all, I reasoned, maybe it was an opportunity for them to get to know their aunts, uncles, grandparents and cousins. Dora scowled at me from the chair, a look of spiteful resentment crossing her face. She was clearly not right.

'Term ends in about ten days,' I said. 'After that I could bring Carrie and Erin to your place for a week or two and maybe help out. We can try to fix things together.'

Mum's face broke into a grin. 'Can we stay here until then?' she asked.

I nodded. This felt completely alien and yet a closer family was something I had always wanted. Maybe this was an opportunity to make it work.

'All right,' I said slowly. 'I'll sleep with Jude and you two can have my bed.'

Jude and David decided they didn't want to come to Wales with us. At seventeen and sixteen, they were old enough to stay in the flat on their own, so I agreed. I think Jude had some vague childhood memories of her grandmother, none of them particularly pleasant, and she had been shocked while I was at work to overhear Dora making a long-distance call on my phone to a friend of hers in Australia.

'You can't do that in someone else's house!' she objected.

Dora was unresponsive and my mother did nothing.

I dreaded the thought of the phone bill when Jude told me, but put it to the back of my mind.

'I don't understand why you're going, Mum,' Jude said. 'What have they ever done for us?'

'You know what it was like when we needed help and no one came forward? We're not like that.'

By contrast, Carrie and Erin were happy to come with me so ten days later we caught the train to Prestatyn. They thought it was another of our mystery adventures and chatted happily on the way.

'Come on, Gran,' Carrie trilled, 'how many sheep can you see in the time it takes me to count to twenty?'

My mother was completely unused to this kind of thing and showed very little interest. She simply wasn't a maternal woman, but I still hoped that she would take to her two lovely granddaughters once she got to know them.

'Which way's the sea?' Erin asked, but Mum ignored her.

I settled back in my seat with Dora still eyeing me up and down. One thing was sure – it was set to be an interesting few days.

We got to my mother's house late that evening and went straight to bed. The next morning we walked over to Dora's place. The first thing that hit me when the door opened was the overpowering smell. Dora had at least a dozen Siamese cats and piles of their food were lying rotting on the sofa cushions while they had used bundles of Dora's laundry as a litter tray. The place stank. Then two St Bernard dogs loped down the hallway, drooling. I love animals but this place was an unsanitary menagerie. It had gotten completely out of hand.

Dora nodded us into the kitchen and out of the back window I saw two big geese in the tiny back yard. As soon they saw us in the kitchen they aggressively flapped their wings to mark their territory.

'We'd better clean this place up for a start, Mum,' I sighed. I felt as though I had done more than my fair share of cleaning up unhygienic houses in the past but there was nothing for it but to muck in.

Mum nodded and I began to roll up my sleeves and head for the kitchen sink. As I passed her, Dora shoved me roughly. Erin stared in horror with her mouth open.

It took several hours but slowly we began to get to the bottom of it. Part of me liked the fact that Mum and I were working together. We had never shared anything before. Dora retreated, scowling, into a back room and we got on with the job.

'We'll need to get at this again tomorrow,' I said.

Mum nodded. However, the next morning she announced she had her own chores to do and I had to set out for Dora's on my own. When I returned home at teatime with the girls she didn't even seem pleased to see us, but I was still determined to help as best I could and I hoped it would help Mum and me to get a bit closer in the process.

On the third day I got in touch with the social worker who had been dealing with Dora's case. My sister had a terrible reputation as a troublemaker and the social work department had all but shelved her case. She threw things at kids in the street and made wild accusations when she was restrained. No doctor in the area was prepared to take her on as a patient.

The social worker was kind but up to her eyes with work. 'I've spoken to the doctor who last had Dora's case. She took him to court for malpractice. It was outrageous.'

'There must be something we can do,' I said to the lady.

'You could try to organize services in a different jurisdiction. Like a fresh start,' she replied. 'But it might be difficult. Dora has caused a lot of trouble.'

We chatted about this for a while and in the end she kindly agreed to investigate the possibilities.

Meanwhile, at least Dora's house looked and smelled a lot better.

'Let's take Carrie and Erin to the park,' I suggested to my mother.

'I have to go to the post office,' she said. 'I have a birthday present to post for one of Lily's kids.' I hadn't seen my youngest sister, Lily, for almost sixteen years. The last time had been the day when I came to Mum's looking for help and Roger came after me; Lily had kindly taken the kids upstairs out of the way. My mother suddenly looked at me. 'Judy, I've just realized that I've never sent your kids birthday or Christmas presents,' she said.

I smiled. This was exactly the kind of realization that might help to reconcile us. 'Just taking them to the park would be great,' I suggested.

But instead my mother went to post the parcel and once more I couldn't help but feel let down. It crossed my mind she might pick something up for the girls while she was in town, but at tea-time she came back empty-handed.

'Will you check on Dora tomorrow?' she asked, and I realized with a sinking heart, that she simply wanted a dogsbody to help out. She had no more interest in my children than she had ever had in me. It felt horrible. I was used to rejection myself but I felt so disappointed for them. It would have been lovely for them to have a proper grandmother, someone else apart from me to care about them in the world, but it was not to be. My hopes of forging a new bond with Mum were all but dashed.

Over the next few days I finished my cleaning at Dora's. She never warmed towards me one bit and was jealous of anyone who took even a small part of our mother's attention. Every day when I turned up the house was messy again and she made no attempt to clean things up herself. The animals roamed freely and every room was a toilet for them. I tried to chat to Dora about it but she spat at me in reply and when she did talk she was aggressive and nonsensical. It reminded me of my father in a rage and I was never sure what she was going to do next. This was my sister, only two years older than me, but I felt no bond towards her and it was clear that she absolutely hated me and didn't want me or the girls in her house.

My mother continued to be cold towards Erin and Carrie and they soon gave up trying to include her in their games. This was not what I had hoped for from the trip and quickly I began to feel used. The atmosphere at my mother's house was unwelcoming and unpleasant and I knew she was only going through the motions and that there was no real warmth in her welcome. One day one of the neighbours arrived to help in the garden and my mother jumped up and gave her a hug. I realized that she simply didn't feel that way about us – she never would – and it hurt.

When the social worker got in touch again and said she had organized some help for Dora in the neighbouring county I handed things over to Mum.

'I'm going back to Sheerwater,' I announced.

There was no point in me staying any longer.

Mum looked slightly put out. 'Whatever you want,' she said in an aloof tone.

As I boarded the train to London I felt a huge wave of disappointment. The trip had been a missed opportunity for us all. I had done my best but things were so one-sided that it was impossible to continue.

'Bye then,' my mother said sullenly.

And as the train pulled away from the platform I finally admitted to myself that we would never bond. I felt completely disillusioned.

'That's that,' I decided. There was no point in bashing my head off a brick wall trying to create an extended family with people who didn't want to know.

The trip to Wales wasn't a complete waste of time, though. Somehow I think it allowed me to step away from the unresolved business of my childhood and move on to something completely new. There were some big plans brewing inside me and now I felt the time was ripe to act on them.

# Chapter Twenty-five

*I*n the autumn of 1982 my older children were becoming more independent and taking confident steps away from me. Jude had always wanted to go to drama school so she was over the moon when she was accepted for a two-year course in Guildford. Once David finished school the following year he too became a student there, and music was his forte. We had many hilarious evenings with the pair of them writing and performing their own comedy songs, which would reduce me to stitches every time.

Helping Jude and David with their drama and theatre studies, and visiting their drama school to watch performances stirred something inside me. I felt that maybe drama could be a useful medium for me too and a possible future vocation. It seemed to me that drama and life have much in common – life means experiencing and then communicating and that was something I had had a problem with since I was a child. I realized that drama could be used to help children to communicate and prepare for adulthood – even children for whom the world was a sad and dangerous place.

I had always felt inferior and isolated as a child. It was difficult to communicate what had happened to me and I remained more of a silent observer than someone who was able to open up. Silence, after all, was safe. Sometimes it was as if there was a mass of words in my mouth and they were choking me, but I couldn't let them out because the sound of my own voice frightened me. No child should ever experience that fear or feel that pain. I now knew that a locked world of silence and suppressed emotions had painful, lifelong consequences. I was well into my thirties and only just beginning to recognize who I was. I'd never told my children about what happened to me in childhood; it felt like too much of a burden to put on them while they were still finding their own way in the world.

Helping kids in similar situations to mine would be a worthwhile objective and I was excited at the prospect. The only problem was that I had left school with no qualifications, and I knew that to be recognized as a teacher I would have to get some before anyone was likely to take my theories seriously.

Despite the fact that I already had two cleaning jobs and two young children still at home, I was determined. I enrolled Carrie, Erin and myself into part-time classes at the same Guildford school as Jude and David. I studied hard for my London Academy of Music and Dramatic Art Teacher's Diploma, which meant taking three examinations in one year. It was really hard work, and at times I had no money for the return train fare and had to walk from Woking to Guildford for classes one evening a week. The weather was often dreadful and the walk took almost three hours. My leg ached horribly with the old injury from those stupid yellow boots I wore when riding in the Globe in Beirut playing up in the cold. Then halfway through term my shoes gave out and I had to patch them up with pieces of cardboard. But it was all worth it.

The class took the form of a series of exercises. One day we had to summon up anger and scream and shout at a pillow.

'Think of something that has made you really angry,' our teacher said, 'and then revert to that to express the emotion.'

The girl next to me muttered 'traffic wardens' but I had deeper resources than that. The pillow became my father and I really let rip.

'That's good, Judy,' the teacher said as my chest heaved after I had finished.

It felt amazing. I never once questioned that I was doing the right thing taking this route. I didn't care how far I had to walk to get there – at least I had enough money for a single ticket home at the end of the night.

The fees for the final exam were really steep, and I made the difficult decision to sell the kitchen table to raise the money so I could travel to London. I recycled part of Carrie's Halloween costume to make the black practice skirt that was required. If I passed this exam I would be able to start teaching and begin to help those children who were really in need

'Good luck, Mum!' the kids shouted from the balcony as I left.

I'd been to LAMDA's Mac Owen Theatre before to take other exams so I was familiar with the set-up. I sat in the dressing room waiting to be called and hoping against hope that I'd be good enough that day to get on the first rung of the ladder. I had to perform monologues by classical playwrights, a couple of modern pieces, some Shakespeare, speeches of verse and prose, improvisation, and also submit written essays and lesson plans. As I ran through my repertoire the examiners took copious notes. At the end of the day I was totally exhausted.

The two weeks before the letter from LAMDA arrived seemed to last forever, then the postman knocked one morning with a huge envelope that wouldn't fit through the letterbox. I walked into the living room where four expectant faces stared at me.

'Go on then, Mum, open it up,' Jude urged.

I opened the letter and read the contents. Knowing that all eyes were on me I didn't change my expression until I closed the envelope, then with a downcast look I said with a sigh, 'No, I didn't pass. Not good enough.'

'Oh, Mum,' they chorused sympathetically, coming over to hug me.

'Gotcha,' I cried, jumping up with a huge grin and waving the envelope up in the air. 'I passed with honours!'

The kids went wild, bouncing around the room.

'Do you get letters after your name now?' David wanted to know.

'Sure do, kiddo.'

David took my letter and certificate and read out 'A.L.A.M. L.L.A.M. (Honours) Member of Association of LAMDA Teachers,' and at that mouthful we all fell on the floor laughing.

I thought back to the teachers at Barnato Park School in South Africa who had always looked down on me. I could still hear the spiteful words Mrs Schmidt, our Afrikaans teacher, addressed to me one day: 'You, madam, will amount to nothing.'

'Says who?' I thought defiantly as I put the certificate away.

That night in bed my mind worked overtime. Now I had a new dream: to open my own drama school.

# Chapter Twenty-six

*I* wanted to set up in an area where resources were low and there were few after-school activities for local children and I didn't have to look very far. My own area of Sheerwater fitted the bill perfectly. Deprivation and poverty in our run-down council estate were rife. The local youth club was struggling to survive, and offered no programmes to keep youngsters interested. The only place where kids could meet was by the row of shops where we lived. After school each day they crammed onto the steps leading up to the flats, drinking and smoking and creating mayhem. Every morning we had to step over condoms, abandoned syringes and all kinds of rubbish. No one seemed to care.

The leader of the youth club agreed that I could rent the hall for one afternoon a week, starting straight after the next school holidays so that my term times corresponded with those of the local schools'. Now I just needed to get the classes advertised so that people knew they were there.

I couldn't afford to pay for ads in the local press, so I took on another cleaning job to provide us with the materials we needed to make posters and flyers. The kids and I sat at the table each evening working on them together. Jude created the posters while Carrie, Erin and I made the flyers, and David designed our logo. I'd decided on the name Gemini Drama Studio, because of the astrological image of twins; while acting, you could be one person on the outside and another inside.

Then we had to deliver the flyers and posters by hand to all the houses, schools, the library, shops, even the local pubs, anywhere we could think of. We traipsed around for days.

I knew I probably wouldn't make any money because all the families in the area were in the same boat as me financially, but that didn't matter. I wasn't in it for the money. To begin with, I suggested that participants just made a small donation to cover costs. The night before I was due to open the school I made a special tea to thank the kids, and we all had a glass of fizzy lemonade to celebrate our new venture.

The next day I waited anxiously inside the hall. I had no idea if anyone would turn up. I straightened the books yet again, and put a record on the turntable. After a couple of minutes the door opened and in walked two little girls aged about five or six, with their mother. It felt as though the sun had suddenly come out after a rainy afternoon. I was so pleased to see them.

'Hello', I beamed. 'How nice to meet you.'

A class of two was smaller than I'd hoped for but we had fun doing dance, mime and improvisation. I wanted to encourage the kids to free up and express themselves. It was hard work keeping them stimulated and I was totally exhausted by the time their mother came to collect them, but they enjoyed themselves immensely and promised to be back the following week.

I wondered as I trudged wearily home just how many would turn up the following week? It was a lot of work for just two students. I needn't have worried. The next week the girls brought some of their friends and from then on the word spread. It wasn't long before we were fully subscribed and had to schedule more classes.

I looked forward to working with the kids and prepared my lessons carefully. As a child the worst sounds I ever heard came from the mouths of adults, so I was always very conscious of how I spoke to the children. My main aim was to give them an enjoyable lesson filled with fun. Many of the kids had communication difficulties, and for one reason or another felt lost in any activities that required participation. I recognized those traits immediately and observed each one closely. I reflected on what had affected me as a lost child, remembering the things that had stunted my ability to grow. Recognizing these traits I was able to devise ways to reach out to the children in my class.

One little girl always hung around the fringes of the group and sat alone on the radiator. Gentle coaxing could not encourage her to take steps forward. Anna's mother had told me how worried she was about her daughter, who had been deeply traumatized after she witnessed her father committing suicide. She was only six and had not uttered a word for months.

My heart went out to this little mite and I thought a great deal about what I could do to help. I asked Erin if I could borrow her teddy bear, and that week during Anna's class I used the teddy as a ventriloquist's doll to talk to the other kids sitting in the circle. Anna sat on the radiator as usual, observing silently. From time to time I threw my voice to her and spoke through the teddy bear.

'Hello,' I said. 'What's your name?'

Then I turned the teddy and talked to the group. I did this several times and could tell I had caught her attention. After a few minutes I finished the exercise and put the teddy to bed. I did this for several sessions, then one day she quietly got down from the radiator and sat next to me. I immediately seized the opportunity to have a story circle.

This is a really good way to get all the kids involved. Each child only has to say one word, but it has to follow on from the last to make a sensible sentence, and as they become more confident these words become a whole story. For children who have difficulties, one word is a huge undertaking. When it came to Anna's turn she froze. I gently put teddy close to her ear and he whispered, 'Not to worry, we'll have another go later.' The story continued but she still couldn't speak. Each time it came round for Anna's turn I sat teddy between us and he offered a word. Then finally, as their story about playing ball developed, she quietly uttered the word 'bat'. The other kids were genuinely delighted that she'd done it. They clapped and cheered. I went over and hugged her and teddy whispered, 'Well done, you clever girl.'

That was the turning point for Anna. She took hold of teddy and wouldn't let him go. Erin agreed to let Anna keep that teddy, which was very generous considering she was only five herself and that teddy was her only toy. Anna continued to come to class every week, and always brought Ted with her. She went on to take her LAMDA exams in acting and years later, catching sight of me from a bus, she leapt off shouting my name and ran over the road to give me a hug.

\* \* \*

The school became a springboard for many other community projects – homes for the elderly, women's groups and schools; we put on shows together and any money generated went back into the community. I didn't pay myself a salary so I had to keep up my cleaning jobs to make ends meet.

The school became so popular that soon after opening we had a waiting list. In order for it to become more self-supporting I began to charge one pound a lesson. I saved as much of this money as I could to create a bursary scheme for dedicated students who could not afford to pay. We cut costs in other ways too: I wrote and choreographed all the shows; Jude was always the stage manager and general dogsbody, and David designed the sets and created many of the costumes. My days at the Casino du Liban were standing me in good stead for the stage craft I now needed.

At Christmas we put on a community pantomime. Most of the cast were students of the school, but I always invited some members of the different clubs to come and take part. One year I wrote a pantomime called 'Cinderella and Friends' and based it on fairy story and nursery rhyme characters. Jack from 'Jack and Jill' was the hero, and Cinderella the heroine. From the start, I had no doubt in my mind who should play the part of Jack. There was a local child called Kate who, at the age of thirteen, had made a name for herself as a troublemaker. Her school were at their wits end over how to deal with her truancy and had pretty much washed their hands of her. I went to see her mum, a very tired and harassed lady with several small children to look after.

'Kate has never missed a class,' I told her. 'She arrives on time and always does her homework. I'd be pleased if you'd allow her to come for extra rehearsals as I'd really like her to play the part of Jack.'

Tears welled up in her eyes and she began to sob. I put my arms around her not knowing what to say.

'Kate loves your classes,' she said. 'She's always wanted to learn drama, it's her dream – the only thing she looks forward to. She's doing a paper round so she can pay for the lessons. Thank you for giving her a chance.'

A couple of weeks before the show we sent out invitations to everyone we could think of – parents, grandparents, teachers and local councillors. I wanted everyone to see these children in a different light. They had all worked together and had developed a great deal of confidence. The show went fantastically well. Kate's mum sat in the front row with all her other kids, her face just glowing with pride. The headmistress from the local school came up to me after the show.

'I can't believe what I have seen tonight,' she said. 'Kate was amazing. She seems like a different child. Her whole attitude to school has changed. Thank you. I will be recommending your classes to all our children.'

After six months of doing paper rounds to pay for her classes, Kate had proved how committed she was so I agreed that she would become the first student to receive our bursary. She went on to pass her exams and was then accepted at drama school in Guildford to study to become an actress.

A couple of weeks after our pantomime we had a huge surprise. 'Cinderella and Friends' received the award for Best Regional Pantomime for that year. I held up the letter and certificate.

'Look, kids – see what you have achieved! Well done, everyone.'

I was so proud of them all. Each one of them had contributed their best efforts.

I was then invited by Surrey County Council to be their Youth and Community Drama Advisor. This came completely out of the blue and it was the first time I ever earned a proper salary in the UK. I was able to open a bank account and strode proudly into the Abbey National in Woking to set one up. In fact, I was so used to living on pennies that it wasn't long before I opened a savings account too. It was wonderful to be able to relax about money and do something that really fired my interest.

The job involved promoting and teaching drama to different youth organizations and organizing them all to perform in a huge variety show. It was going to be hard work as several hundred children would be involved from all over the county. But it was very worthwhile.

The kids and I skipped home the night of the show singing the song from the finale and I felt as though a new heart was beginning to beat, bringing hope and light to downtrodden Sheerwater, and to me as well.

# Chapter Twenty-seven

Year after year the school's reputation flourished. Our students continued to gain excellent passes in their exams, and many of them went on to have successful careers in the world of entertainment. My greatest joy was receiving news from past students who had blossomed from small frightened children into confident adults able to achieve their goals and become the people they wanted to be.

In my personal life I had very little time to enjoy social activities as all my energy was taken up in caring for my family, teaching and fulfilling my role as Drama Advisor at the County Council. As my children got older they began to show their concerns about me being on my own, although they understood why I preferred it that way. My two disastrous relationships had been more than enough for me. I was much happier by myself and I wanted to devote my life to doing the best for my family.

'There'll be plenty of time for me to think about what I'll do with myself when you've all left home,' I assured them.

But from time to time they came up with other suggestions.

'Mum, why don't you join a club or something? Maybe you'll meet somebody nice?' Jude might suggest.

'Yeah, Mum, someone who'll look after you for a change,' David added, putting his arm around me.

One year on Valentine's Day a card arrived by post. I looked twice to see if it had been delivered to the wrong house. But no, it was addressed to me.

'Who in the world has sent a Valentine card to me?' I wondered.

The card was really pretty with hearts and flowers all over it and an inscription saying, 'With love from Braithwaite xxx.'

Who the heck was Braithwaite?

I received another card on my fortieth birthday. This really puzzled me. Then one day when I was discussing it with the kids, my rogue son gave me a cheeky grin.

'I sent them, Mum. I wanted you to feel special and I didn't want you to think you were forgotten. I don't want to see you on your own when we've all left home. We just want you to have someone in your life.'

'OK, OK,' I said, with mock despair. 'I don't want to meet anyone, but I don't mind writing letters. Will it make you happier if I find myself a pen-pal?'

'That'd be a start,' he replied.

I'd made the pen-pal suggestion to shut them up, but when I gave it a little thought I wondered whether perhaps writing to someone might be interesting. I found a magazine called *Singles* in the newsagents. Inside there were lists of people looking for friends. I searched specifically for someone who only wanted a pen friend – no marriage, no romance, just letters.

My life became a little less hectic in 1984 after the older kids left home. Jude graduated from college and went to work using drama and the arts to benefit the voluntary sector. David, armed with a gold medal for acting, decided to pursue a musical career. Carrie and Erin, now active teenagers, were developing and enjoying their own interests. I was so proud to see them all taking these confident steps into their new worlds. And as this happened, I too began entering a new phase in my life.

I had replied to a number of adverts in *Singles* magazine. Most of them, from the outset, listed their requirements for a long-term relationship, which obviously put me right off. There was one, though, that interested me in particular: 'Scottish man with smallholding, ten hens and a dog, who likes going for walks, seeks pen-pal.'

I liked the simplicity of the image this conjured up so I wrote to him and we got into correspondence.

John's letters were open and warm. I sensed his honesty and this was refreshing. He wrote about his life in the Highlands, just outside Inverness, and it seemed a world away from mine in busy Woking. He loved classical music, and his favourite pastime was to walk his dog in the surrounding hills. This man was at one with nature and for the first time in my life I felt that there was someone who shared my simple philosophy of life. He was gentle in thought, mind and spirit but had a fierce intolerance of injustice.

Soon John became my only pen friend, and I began to look forward keenly to his letters. I was living for the present and didn't burden him with my troubled past. He didn't tell me much about his past either, although he did mention that he'd had a brush with cancer a few years before and had had a kidney removed, an experience that had made him appreciate his simple life and stunning surroundings all the more. Usually we shared our thoughts and feelings about life in general rather than writing about our lives. He seemed to understand me, and over the two years that we wrote to each other we became very close.

We swapped photos at one stage and he looked just the way I had imagined: strong, with a rugged, outdoors kind of appearance and a handsome face, I thought.

One morning in 1987, I was startled to receive a letter from John inviting me up to Inverness to have a holiday with him. I told Carrie and Erin about it over breakfast and they were unanimous in insisting that I should go.

'Go on Mum, you never have a holiday,' Carrie insisted.

'I can't leave you two here on your own, now can I?'

'No, but we can stay at Jude's or David's. They're always asking us to go,' Erin pointed out.

Very tentatively, I began to explore the idea that maybe I might go. Why not? I felt the first flutter of excitement that John had asked me. It may sound naïve but it didn't occur to me for a moment that there might be a romantic subtext. I thought of him as a very close friend and looked forward to our friendship deepening when we met. I didn't have a moment of hesitation about whether I could trust him or not. Over the years of working in community drama I had met all kinds of people and learned to read them. Now I was pretty sure I could trust my own instincts about character and I knew without doubt from John's letters that he was a decent, honest man.

Jude and David agreed to look after the girls, so I wrote to John suggesting a date when I could come and he agreed by return. The night before I left the girls helped me to pack.

'You be a good girl and have fun,' Carrie instructed.

'Yes, we want to know *all* about your adventures when you get back. Don't forget to write it all down in your journal,' Erin teased.

'Don't forget who's the mum round here!' I chided, pretending to give them each a clip on the ear.

When I boarded the train it felt momentous, as though I was entering a whole new era. Here I was, at forty-two, going to stay with a man I had known for two years but never met. No one had ever seemed to understand me as much as John did. I looked forward to getting his letters and loved the fact that we were so in tune with each other. I was excited at the prospect of meeting him in person because for the first time we'd be able to have a proper two-way conversation.

'This is going to be lovely,' I thought to myself.

The scenery on the nine-hour journey to Inverness was breathtaking. It reminded me of the views I had loved in New Zealand. This was something just for me, so I settled down and soaked in the moment. As we got closer I began to picture meeting John. Would it be a crowded station? Would I recognize him from his photo?

The train pulled in and I grabbed my bag, stepped onto the platform and there he was. I recognized him immediately. He had a huge smile on his face.

'Judy!' he said as he hugged me. 'Welcome to Inverness.'

He took my bag and then led me by the hand to his car.

'Let's go for a quiet drink and have a chat before we go home.'

# Chapter Twenty-eight

*A*t a corner table in the dimly lit bar of the hotel, John and I talked for ages. There seemed so much to catch up on. His gentle Scots accent seemed almost melodic and sitting there like that, I felt as though I'd come home. Everything slotted into place.

Before we knew it, it was ten o'clock.

'We'd better get back,' John said, 'you must be tired after your long journey.'

It was still quite light outside, which seemed really strange to me.

'Being so far north,' John explained, 'it hardly gets dark at all in summertime.'

We took a slow drive to where John lived. The winding country roads seemed to stretch for miles, and I was in awe of the surrounding natural beauty. Against the backdrop of the wild rugged hills were lush green fields and rippling streams. Farmhouses dotted about with livestock added to the picture postcard scene. It was an amazing place.

'Here we are then,' John said, as we turned into a very narrow lane.

From his descriptive letters I'd tried to visualize the place he lived, but to witness it first hand was astounding. His little cottage sat nestled in acres of woodland surrounded by a flower-filled garden. It was perfect.

John showed me to a bedroom looking out across the hills and I slept soundly. I woke the next morning to the smell of breakfast cooking. John was in the kitchen, the table was set and coffee ready.

'Good morning, sleep well?' John asked

'Like a log, thank you,' I answered.

It felt a little odd for me to be standing there in a strange kitchen with a man cooking breakfast. I just wasn't used to it. I hovered by the table, but John soon put me at my ease.

'You sit down and help yourself. Would you like some real Scots porridge, just made?' he said.

'No thank you, John. Porridge and me are not the best of friends,' I shuddered slightly. When I was very young, my sisters and I had been looked after by an awful couple called the Epplestones, after Mum had run off with a new man and abandoned us. Every morning, Mrs Epplestone had force-fed me with porridge, yanking back my head and forcing the spoon down my throat, so it was hardly surprising that I'd never taken to porridge thereafter.

'You can't go on our walks today without having a real Highland breakfast. How many eggs would you like?' John asked.

On the table there were about a dozen eggs, bacon, black pudding, white pudding, mushrooms and heaven knows what else.

'There's enough there to feed an army!' I laughed.

'Och aye.' He grinned. 'Us wee Scots are tough and we have to eat hearty.'

He explained that the eggs came from his ten hens, each of which had its own pet name.

'I'm looking forward to meeting your little family,' I said tucking into the biggest breakfast I had ever seen.

'I thought I'd take you to Loch Farr this morning.'

'Is that the place you wrote about, the one that's hidden from view, and you found by accident?'

'That's the one, a real slice of heaven.'

Loch Farr certainly was amazing. From the roadside no one would ever have believed that such a place existed. We had to walk through woods and tiny clearings before we found it, and then suddenly there it was, like walking into another world. The loch stretched out for miles. The sun's rays created prisms of light on the surface making it sparkle. The water was so clear that mirror images of the surrounding hills and woodland brought a dynamic dimension to the picture. We both took a deep breath as we stood and looked in wonder. John took my hand and held it tight. Not a word was said. It didn't seem necessary.

Later, after a long walk we lay on the picnic blanket and chatted. John worked as an inspector for the Health and Safety Executive for Agriculture. It was a very stressful job. He investigated accidents on farms, some of them horrific, and he'd had to deal with several cases of children who'd been mutilated and killed after falling from tractors. He came home after these experiences deeply stressed and worried that more could have been done to make things safer. He'd written to me about a favourite hillside spot where he went to relax.

'Is this the place you told me about?' I asked.

'Sure is,' he said with a smile, 'and I'm happy to be sharing it with you.'

We lay there for hours. Among other things, I told him about a recurring dream I had when I was a kid about having an Indian brave for a friend. John sat up at that.

'I had a dream like that too. I was friends with a little Indian girl. We became blood brothers.'

I stiffened. 'Really?'

'Yes. I used to have that dream all the time.'

I had a strange feeling. It was a weird coincidence. Exactly the same thing happened in my dream. I'd never really understood when people used the term 'soul mate' before, but suddenly it was beginning to make sense.

We spent our days climbing hills and discovering new paths, having picnics by the lochs or just lying in the sun. John was fascinated to hear about all the places I'd seen as he'd always longed to travel. I began to understand that he had led a very quiet and conservative life. This, he admitted, made him cautious about travel.

'I wanted to go to Africa when I was a boy,' he said wistfully. 'I wish that I had gone now.'

He also had a passion for motorbikes, and kept one in his garage, so he was absolutely stunned when I told him that I'd been a stuntwoman riding inside a sixteen-foot diameter metal cage! In the evenings we often sat listening to classical music before walking outside to sit at the foot of a tree and look up at the stars. The more time that John and I spent together the more we realized how at one we were. He was the first person I'd ever met, other than my children, who understood everything I had to say.

All too soon the holiday drew to an end, and on the day before I was due to go home we took Misty, John's dog, to the top of one of the hills. We stood hand in hand sharing the moment, at peace together. John then left me for a minute or two, and when he returned he gently handed me a wild rose. Not a word was said but his eyes were bright with emotion. It was then that we knew we had found each other.

Back at the cottage John put his arms around me and I knew that we were meant to be together.

'I don't want you to go, Judy. Please will you come back soon, and bring the girls next time?'

'I'd like that very much. I'm going to miss you too.'

John didn't want to let me go at the station, and it was a very sad moment for us both as the train pulled out and I saw him disappear into the distance. My journey back to Woking was filled with thoughts of our time together. He had given me something that I had never had in a relationship with a man before. He accepted me for who I was, plain and simple. And to me, simplicity was the key to love. That meant everything.

I'd only been away from Sheerwater a short while but it seemed an age. The kids had had a whale of a time at David's house, and now all four of them wanted to know everything that had happened in Inverness.

'Are you going to tell us or what?' David quizzed.

I grinned and kept them dangling for a while.

'Come on, Mum,' badgered Jude. 'Fill us in.'

'Well,' I said at last. 'There is a man out there who has turned my steely heart into soft soap.'

'Wow! That's fantastic.' They all gathered round and almost knocked me over in their rush for hugs.

'When are you going back?'

We agreed that Carrie and Erin would come back up to Inverness with me in two weeks' time when their term ended, and when John phoned later that evening to check I'd got home safely, he was delighted to hear our plans.

As the time drew nearer the girls became very excited, looking forward to meeting John and seeing Scotland for the first time. I was naturally concerned about how John and the girls would get on. Erin and Carrie were now twelve and fourteen, and as far as they could remember they'd always had me to themselves. I wondered how they would feel with John in the picture? I explained that they were my main priority and if they had any concerns when we were in Scotland they were to let me know.

'Don't worry, Mum,' Carrie said. 'If you like him we know he must be OK.'

On the way up in the train, the girls asked lots of questions.

'He has ten chickens,' I told them, 'and one is called Aggie. She, poor thing, is so hen-pecked that she's hardly got any feathers. The other hens steal her food and so John goes and gives her extra when all the others are out and about.'

I told them how different Inverness was to Woking. 'There are fields and woods as far as the eye can see, and on the road to John's house there's hardly ever another person never mind a car. There are rivers and lochs to swim in, and loads of hills to climb.' It was another world.

John had booked some time off work so that we could have a relaxed couple of weeks. At the station he ran almost the full length of the train to greet us. He wrapped his arms round me and then welcomed the girls.

'I am so happy to meet you two. Your mum has told me so much about you.'

John held my hand as we walked to the car and I took a sly look at Carrie and Erin. They were both grinning.

The first thing the girls wanted to do was meet the ten little hens.

'Aww, poor little Aggie,' said Erin passing over the titbits John had given her. 'Can I feed her every day?'

'Of course,' he smiled.

The girls loved the freedom of the countryside. Every day we walked in the hills, paddled in streams, bathed in the lochs and had picnics. John took us on nature trails and talked to the girls about Highland wildlife. As we shared these times together I could see that he was just as at home with the girls as he was with me. This felt like a place and a person I had been searching for all my life.

A few nights before we were due to leave Inverness I took a walk around the garden to enjoy the cool night air, and as I looked towards the heavens I was taken back to my child-hood. During that dark existence I had thought of the stars as my real family and I looked to them for comfort. In times of desperate need it was their light that gave me hope – a sign that they were still out there looking for me. And there in the garden that night, as if waiting only for me, was a large star resting at the top of the hill. It looked so close that I felt I could almost touch it. I lifted my arm as though to reach it and whispered, 'Thank you for bringing me home.'

'What are you doing all alone out here?' John asked, and came and stood beside me. Then he looked up, following my gaze and said, 'Magic, just magic.' He took me by the hand and spoke very gently: 'Let's take a walk up the hill.'

We climbed the slope in the darkness and sat on a rock at the top to enjoy the view.

'Judy, I want to ask you something very important,' he began cautiously. 'How would you feel about coming back soon and staying here for good?'

'You want us to come and live with you?'

'We're meant to be together. We're like the blood brothers in our dreams. I love you. Judy, please will you marry me?'

As he looked into my eyes for my answer, a tear rolled down his cheek. The man I loved had asked me to marry him. I held his face in my hands, kissing away his tears as mine fell. I whispered, 'I would be honoured to marry you, John. Yes.'

I was the luckiest woman in the world.

# Chapter Twenty-nine

I t may sound strange that I felt so sure when I had only spent a short time with John, but we knew all we needed to know about each other from two years of correspondence. I'd had one husband who tried to control me completely and another who was a child and needed to be looked after. This time I knew I'd found someone who would be an equal, a partner who would encourage and support me. But above and beyond any practicalities, I had fallen in love for the first time – real romantic love, quite different from what I felt for my children. It was a complete revelation to me and I sometimes had to stop and pinch myself, afraid it was just a dream. How could something quite so wonderful have happened to little Judy at the ripe old age of forty-two?

That night we went back to the cottage to celebrate our engagement with a glass of wine and we stayed up late making plans. I would go back to Woking to hand in my notice on the flat, pass on my drama classes to Rita, one of my mature students, and organize for Carrie and Erin to transfer to a school in Inverness. It was almost September but I reckoned I could pack everything up and be back in a month.

I was worried that Carrie and Erin might not want to move to the Highlands, but they couldn't have been more delighted when we told them the news the next morning.

'What have I been saying all along, Mum?' Carrie said. 'That you two should be together. You're peas in a pod!'

Erin surprised me by saying she would like to stay with John in Inverness while Carrie and I went back to Woking to pack things up. I couldn't have asked for a more eloquent expression of the way she trusted him right from the start.

This time when John waved us off at the station, I waved back happily because I knew it wouldn't be long before we were together again.

Back in Woking I phoned Jude and David with the news and they were both absolutely delighted. We arranged that they could come up for a visit to meet John in October once I was back there. I handed in my notice on the flat and gave away my furniture to a family in need. My student Rita was as pleased as punch when I asked if she would like to take over my drama classes and I knew I was leaving them in safe hands.

Four weeks after we left Inverness, Carrie and I stood for a few moments looking round the empty flat. It was exciting to realize that once we closed the door behind us we were embarking on a new chapter in our lives and this time I had no fears or reservations. Jude was coming to drive us to the station and when we heard her honking downstairs, we picked up our bags and headed off.

Back in Inverness, things moved very quickly. The night I got back, John asked 'How would you like to be married right here in front of the fire?'

A very simple celebration appealed to us both, so we rang Harriet, a lady minister friend of John's elderly aunt.

'I'd be delighted to officiate your cottage wedding,' she told John. 'I have a free date on the eleventh of November . How would that do?'

November the eleventh it was – just a few weeks away.

'Let's not tell the kids,' I said. 'Let's keep it as a surprise.'

In the meantime I had plenty to do. John knew nothing about drama or theatre but he was always interested in my work, and when I suggested opening a school in Inverness he was encouraging.

'There's a community centre in the town. I'll make some enquiries for you,' he offered.

The Spectrum Centre was an ideal place. Neil Thomson, the youth and community leader, was happy with the idea of a theatre school in Inverness.

Arrangements were made and I announced that I would open in January.

Every evening John and I took the dog for a walk in the woods, and as Misty ran around sniffing for rabbits we sat by our favourite tree. Sitting between the massive roots it felt as though the tree had wrapped protective arms around us. I felt safe and cared for in a way I never had throughout my life to that date. It was the perfect way to end the day.

As we sat there on 10 November, the evening before our wedding, John took out a little box and gave it to me. I opened it to find a beautiful silver locket, and inside were two tiny photographs, one of him and the other of me. He took it out and helped me put it on.

'Your 'something new' for tomorrow,' he whispered.

After breakfast the next morning we waved the girls off to school and as they left John gave me a wink. They still had no idea of the planned celebrations for later that afternoon.

Harriet was travelling from Fife that morning. It was going to be a very private ceremony, with just four close family members present – Carrie, Erin, John's son Jamie and his girlfriend Jackie – and a few friends for the party afterwards. Unfortunately neither Jude nor David could get leave from work to be with us on the day, but promised to make up for it at a later date.

When Carrie and Erin came home from school that afternoon they immediately noticed the table set with food.

'What's going on?' asked Erin.

Carrie looked around thoughtfully and then asked, 'Is this what I think it is?'

'Yes, my lovely, Harry is here to marry John and me, and you two will be our guests of honour.'

Both girls dashed off to get changed into some party gear.

John arrived home with Jamie and Jackie, who had agreed to be our witnesses. Jamie was a gamekeeper at a lodge not far from where we lived. He was a gentle boy, very much like his dad. John's other son, Angus, was working down south but he phoned and sent some beautiful flowers.

At 6 o'clock on the dot we were all ready. Harry was dressed in her ceremonial robes. She stood next to the girls, who were both looking glamorous. Jamie and Jackie took their places behind John and me, and Misty the dog lay in front of the fire, oblivious.

Harry made it a very special and loving service, and as she pronounced us husband and wife and John placed the ring on my finger, she was visibly moved. At the end John took me into his arms and held me tightly.

'Together at last,' I whispered.

'Forever,' he replied.

That night, much later than usual, when everyone had left, John and I walked to the top of the hill. It seemed almost magical to be enveloped in the gentle stillness of the night. We stood hand in hand in the moonlight then John took me in his arms and as we whispered our own special vows, a soft winter breeze rustled through the trees carrying our words away as if in celebration.

# Chapter Thirty

The Highland winter set in with a vengeance. The girls and I had never experienced such cold and frosty weather. All over Christmas and New Year we were snowed in, our little cottage hardly visible as the drifts reached past the windowsills. We had hilarious times trying to walk the dog because the snow went over the top of our Wellington boots, grounding us so that we couldn't move an inch. After a few steps, we would inevitably fall over, laughing, into a snowdrift.

The new drama school was set to open in mid-January and it looked as though we were going to be busy. There was a flood of enquiries and requests to enrol, and I already had enough students to open three classes a week.

I came up with a name for the new school after a strange dream I had one night. John and I liked sharing our dreams so I described it to him: 'I was caring for a hundred lost and frightened children. There was a tremendous electric storm and the children were crying. I needed to get them to a place of safety. Then, from out of nowhere a pure white Pegasus flew over us. He carried us on his wings to a beautiful garden.' I paused. 'So I've decided to call it The Pegasus Theatre School. What do you think?'

'That seems very fitting,' John smiled.

He took a keen interest in my work but although he fully supported my passion for helping children, he never knew my deep-rooted reasons for doing so. I was determined that what had happened to me would never tarnish the people I loved and so I never told him about my childhood. The present was what mattered to both of us.

The school was important to me and it grew from strength to strength. Soon I had three hundred students and was taking twelve classes a week. As with all my other schools the main priority was for the children to gain confidence. The money from fees and performances went to help the less fortunate and I encouraged a wide variety of charitable projects. One of the biggest thrills for the children was adopting ten whales. I had written a musical portraying man from the perspective of animals, called 'Hear their Voices'. The show was hugely successful and the money we raised allowed us to adopt ten whales, because their plight was urgent at the time. Every year we received a report on them and it was great for the kids to feel so involved.

I also started giving free classes to physically and mentally disabled youngsters, and many students wishing to take Theatre Arts professionally came to study. We needed to go to London at least three times a year for examinations. Lots of our students had never been outside Inverness never mind as far as London, so after their exams at LAMDA we went to a West End musical as a celebration. This was great fun, and my students sang the songs from the shows through the streets on their way back to the hostel where we were staying.

I was also invited to teach at two primary schools – Farr Primary just down the road from where we lived, and Whitebridge, which was some distance away.

'You'll need transport to get there,' John said. 'You'd better take the motorbike.'

This was fantastic. I hadn't ridden a motorbike since my stunt motorcycle days. I often wondered what the local Highland folk thought of a middle-aged English woman scooting down their country lanes on a 500cc motorbike. I was very tempted to pull a wheelie, but I knew that would look like showing off!

'I wish I could have come to your school when I was a kid,' John said as we walked through the woods one evening about a year after we were married.

His own childhood had been very restrained – fun was not on the agenda.

'It's wonderful to see the kids leaving your classes full of hope that everything is possible. I feel as if I haven't done everything I wanted to. I used to read this comic about a World War II airline pilot. I'd have loved to be able to fly a plane like him.'

As he spoke a plan began to form in my mind.

'Are you sure you want a part-time cleaning job?' John asked the next day when I announced my intentions.

'It's just to earn a little extra for those unexpected expenses,' I said. 'I have time in the morning. I might as well make good use of it.'

John was happy with that explanation and so I worked for a few weeks to save up enough money for my plan to work.

In February 1990, the day before John's 45th birthday, I asked him to take us to the airport, claiming that Erin had some research to do for a school project. The girls were both in on the secret.

As we approached the airport, I said: 'Just before you get to that gate, John, could you just stop the car for a moment?'

He looked puzzled but did as I asked.

'We're going to play a birthday game, so please put this blindfold on.'

'What are you up to now?' John quizzed a little cautiously.

We took him by the hand and led him to an area where a plane was waiting, with an instructor standing beside it. I took off the blindfold and we all shouted 'Happy Birthday'. John was speechless. His face was a picture.

'Go and have fun,' I said hugging him, 'and fly as high as your World War II hero. I've booked you a couple of flying lessons.'

On the way home from the airport John was like a kid. 'It was fabulous, amazing!' he said. 'We flew right over the house!'

Erin and I couldn't get a word in edgeways!

During 1990 John's workload became increasingly heavy. There were many accidents to inspect and he was tired and began to suffer from debilitating headaches. He took to wandering off on his own and I often had to go out and look for him. Usually I found him in one our remote places just sitting and staring into space. I sat next to him holding him close while he seemed lost in a world of pain. He lay with his head on my lap and when he felt ready to speak he just said, 'It's been a rotten day.'

Most worryingly, he began to get irritable over tiny things, and then he'd become impatient and sometimes unreasonably angry. I knew these were classic stress symptoms. His moods were normal for a while and then without warning became erratic again. This really scared me. At these times he almost seemed to be someone else. It reminded me of my father, of course, though I never told him that. I knew, deep down, that this was not John. He would never hurt me. I just felt that the pressure and stress of work was getting to him. I began to formulate another plan that I hoped might help him feel better.

To earn the extra money to put my new plan into action I took on two more cleaning jobs. After months of hard graft I managed to save up enough just in time for Christmas. On Christmas Eve I gave John a plain white envelope. The girls were so excited they could hardly sit still.

'Merry Christmas, love,' I said.

John was always delighted to receive gifts. It wasn't something he'd been much used to in his childhood. He was mystified by this one though. He opened the envelope and took out a picture of an elephant, a giraffe, a lion and a hippo and by the time he'd got to the monkey he was utterly confused.

'Do you like it?' I asked.

'Yes, but what is it?'

The girls were about to explode when I said, 'Oh, silly me, I've left part of it in the bedroom.'

I brought out the rest of the present – tickets and safari brochures. A huge smile lit up John's face.

'Is this what I think it is?' he asked cautiously.

The girls couldn't contain themselves any longer as they blurted out, 'You're going to Africa!'

It was another of John's dreams and I hoped an exotic holiday would do him good.

\* \* \*

We flew to Mombassa in time for John's forty-sixth birthday in February 1991. It was good to see my husband feeling more cheerful and back to his old self, though his headaches continued. It was the first time in his life he had travelled so far abroad, and on our first evening as we walked barefoot along the beach he was in tears as he said, 'I dreamt of this as a boy, and now I'm here.'

John loved Africa, especially the wildlife, but was very concerned about the poverty and deprivation of the people. With his health and safety expertise, he was appalled when he saw a local farm worker pouring chemicals onto a grass verge, barefoot.

'I'm giving that man my shoes,' he said. And true to his word, he did.

As a special treat I booked a few days at the Aberdares National Park, and we stayed in the famous Treetops Hotel, where the young Elizabeth Windsor was staying in 1952 the night she heard that her father had died and she was to become Queen of England. The hotel rose up from the ground on stilts and overlooked two water holes. Mount Kenya was in full view and the bush was breathtaking.

Each morning John got up early with his camera to wait for the animals to come to the waterholes and bathe.

'Judy, look, there're four elephants just splashing about in the water. I can't believe we are so close to them.'

In the evenings little monkeys came to the dinner table and tried to pinch bits off our plates. Most of all, we were both looking forward to the night safari. A ranger armed with a rifle took us through the bush. We sat on a hilltop and surveyed the landscape by the light of an artificial moon that they had set up – a huge, illumination that wouldn't scare the wildlife. Elephants and buffalo tramped past along their routes, unaware they were being watched.

Another day we went to a small African village to watch local dancing, visit their well, have a meal and sample the local beer. We had a fabulous day. I was given an enormous snake to handle. It sat around my neck for ages and fell fast asleep. And the beer tasting was an experience! The cup had a piece of muslin around the top, and we had to drink the beer through it to stop us swallowing the bugs and insects that were floating inside.

'I think I'll stick to Tennent's lager,' said John, pulling a face.

At the end of the day he was exhausted and as I cuddled his head on my lap he whispered, 'You're right, you know. Everything is possible.'

It was a wonderful trip but I was becoming increasingly alarmed about John's health. He was usually so fit, but now he seemed to be losing mobility in his left hand and foot, and he wasn't aware of it. He had difficulties walking down a hill one day and then in the dining room he didn't notice that he wasn't holding his tray properly and all the food fell to the floor. He got headaches that did not respond to painkillers and during the last few days in Mombassa he mostly slept. Things were clearly not right and I wanted to get him safely home as soon as possible.

The journey back to Scotland was in stark contrast to the excitement of coming out to Kenya. John was very nervous, almost frightened of the plane, and travelling back on the train his behaviour became irrational. I had to keep reassuring him that we were on the way home and he would soon be in his own bed.

I tried to suppress them, but alarm bells were ringing in my head. Something was terribly wrong. This wasn't just a bit of stress. This was something more serious.

# Chapter Thirty-one

$O$nce we got home John relaxed a little.

'I think it's best if we phone Doctor Bennett and see about these headaches of yours,' I suggested.

'I know I'm not right, and I just want the pains to go away,' he replied in a whisper.

Luckily, living in a rural area the doctor came to visit us so we didn't need to attend a surgery. Dr Bennett was almost at retirement age, an extremely nice man and very professional. He was more of a friend than the local GP. After a basic examination Dr Bennett took out his torch to look behind John's eyes. I could tell by his face that it was bad news. My throat felt dry.

'You need further investigation, John,' he said slowly. 'You'll need to go to hospital for that I'm afraid. I'll set it up. And Judy, if you need me for anything you know where I am.'

We went to the hospital together. John was terrified. He only had to stay a few days, but he had a severe hospital phobia and hated being there.

'Please don't leave me,' he begged.

I loathed having to leave him and visited as often as could, staying most of the day. I arranged that the students

I had been teacher training would take over my classes for a while so that I could give John one hundred percent of my attention. I just wanted him back home with me again. I missed him very badly.

At long last we were called into the specialist's office. 'I am afraid the news isn't good,' he said with concern in his voice. 'The cancer you had years ago has metastasized and spread widely through your body, and you now have an inoperable tumour on the brain.'

My heart jumped into my throat. I couldn't believe what he was saying. I knew that John was ill, and I'd imagined that maybe he'd need an operation or something but never had it occurred to me it would be so serious. This was the worst scenario I could ever imagine. I don't think I took it all in that day because of the overwhelming shock.

'We can help relieve some of the pain by giving you radiotherapy and steroid tablets,' the doctor continued gently. 'But I'm afraid your prognosis is not good.'

I looked at John and he looked at me. His face contorted and tears were welling in his eyes. I put my arm around him and held his hand. We were both shaking. After a minute or so John looked up.

'How long do I have?'

'Six months maximum, John. I'm so sorry.'

He was forty-six.

As though through a fog, I heard the doctor say that when he became weaker John would need hospital care. For now they wanted to keep him one more night. Back on the ward, I sat with him till he fell asleep. Neither of us could find any words. I suppose it didn't seem real. It takes a while for your mind to process such devastating news.

As I walked down the corridor to leave, I felt trapped in a nightmare. The doctor's words echoed round my head and the word 'NO' was screaming at me. I got into the lift and a nurse who knew our case got in behind me.

'Are you alright?' she asked.

I couldn't answer. Tears filled my eyes. The man I loved was going to die. I repeated the words in my head, trying to make sense of them. It was so cruel. We should have had so much life in front of us, so many more experiences to share.

Alone in our bed that night I cried and cried for us both – for the harshness of having all your dreams come true one moment and then having them snatched away again the next. For the fact that it was so unfair that John would miss out on decades of life he should have had. For the girls, who already adored him. And for me. That night was tough, but by morning I was determined that I would dedicate myself to making his last six months as happy as I could. There was to be no sadness here. We were going to live every minute of our time together.

When John came home from the hospital we went to our favourite place by the river and swore our love for each other, then and for always. We sat for ages on a picnic blanket and took a photograph on John's time-release camera to mark that special day. I still have it. We're smiling and tanned from our time in Africa, he's got his arm round me, and you can't see from our expressions that we've just been struck such a huge blow. We look like any couple who are passionately in love.

# Chapter Thirty-two

*I*t took quite a while before John and I came to terms with what we had been told. We were so involved with hospital appointments and medication schedules that we had little time to share our innermost thoughts and feelings. Maybe it would have been too hard to talk intimately. I just wanted to be strong for him and make things as easy as possible, so part of that involved protecting him from witnessing my distress.

There were a lot of people we needed to tell. John's work colleagues were badly shocked and they arranged a party to wish him well. Afterwards as John left the building he looked really tired. He took my hand with a deep sigh and said, 'Let's get home and see the girls.'

Erin was living with us and Carrie was up on holiday for a few days when we heard the news and they were both devastated. To them John was now their dad, and they loved him. John's own sons were also distraught when he broke the news.

Dr Bennett knocked on the kitchen door ashen-faced as soon as he received the news about John's prognosis from the hospital.

'I am so sorry,' he said.

We were both touched that he had made the long trip to our house just to express his concern.

'Come on in,' I said. 'Let's have a glass of wine.'

Neither of us wanted to dwell on the medical details, so we told him all about our trip to Kenya and John showed him his photographs.

'You are going to make the best of this, I can see,' the doctor said as he left.

We were certainly going to try.


The radiotherapy and medication did help. John had much more energy – in fact he seemed to have bounds of it. He was up at the crack of dawn not wanting to miss a moment of the day. The steroid tablets also gave him a huge appetite, and he put on quite a bit of weight. He was still able to laugh when he lost the little hair he had left due to the radiotherapy.

'How do you like the flies' ballroom up top?' he said patting his bald head.

He liked to dabble with a paintbrush and often left the house in the early hours to go and find an early morning scene to paint.

Those months were very special for us. We knew that the treatments were only temporary aids, but they gave us some much-treasured time to say goodbye.

While John was feeling reasonably well I went back to taking some classes at the school. I had many students who were due to take their exams in June and wanted to make sure they were on track. Between sessions I went to the library and read as much as I could about caring for a terminally ill patient. There was so much I needed to know.

John had begged me not to send him to hospital again when he became worse, and I had promised him faithfully that I would care for him at home. Dr Bennett knew what we were planning and said he'd help as much as he could.

One day I came across an article saying cancer researchers had found a new drug. I immediately telephoned the hospital and made an appointment with John's specialist, hope springing that maybe it might help John. The doctor chatted to me for over an hour and explained that it wasn't the right kind of medication for John's specific case, but I was still glad I had gone to find out. I needed to know that we had done everything possible. If there was a single thing I could have done – anything at all – there's no question that I would have done it.

I was worried about leaving John when it was exam time. I was scheduled to take my students to London and he insisted that I go ahead. It was only for two days and Erin was there to look after him.

The students all passed with flying colours but I rushed home anxious to see that everything was OK, and was greeted by John standing up a ladder. He had painted the whole cottage when I was away.

'Waste of time trying to be nurse round here,' Erin said with a grin. 'He's almost as stubborn as you are!'

At the beginning of July 1991 John's deterioration began and it escalated fast. He became very quiet, almost insular, and his physical mobility deteriorated. One day as we walked in town he was unaware that he was walking with one foot in the gutter and one on the pavement. He lost the ability to speak, which he found hugely frustrating. Soon grunting became his only communication. It all happened so fast there was almost no time to mourn for the long conversations we used to have about anything and everything. I just kept taking care of the practicalities.

Then, one day when I went out shopping I left John sitting comfortably on the sofa. 'I won't be long, love,' I said. 'I've just got to go and get some groceries. I'll be back in no time at all.'

I jumped on the motorbike and dashed to the shops. When I got home John had disappeared. I searched the house. Just as I was about to launch a full-scale search outside, I heard a muffled sound coming from behind the sofa. I moved it and found John on the floor, unable to find his way out. He must have tried to get up and fallen. It was awful to see him so helpless but it was only set to get worse.

A few days later I was in the garden putting out rubbish when I heard a crash from the bathroom. John was lying on his back on the floor, unconscious. When he came round he was frightened and had no idea how he had got there or what had happened. It was then that I knew I would have to confine him to bed for his own safety.

I took him to the bedroom and put him to bed but he became very agitated and I realized he didn't want to be stuck there. So I took one of the single beds from the spare room and set it up in the lounge where he was more in the centre of the household and could see Erin and me coming and going. This time he was much more relaxed and fell asleep. From then on I slept on the sofa in case he needed me during the night. I had to keep going for his sake. I couldn't afford the release of tears.

Dr Bennett came every other day. He also arranged for two nurses to visit – one of them from Macmillan Cancer Care – and they were a big help. Although John was unable to communicate, I wanted him to feel as comfortable as possible so I had to try and judge what he needed for myself. Even though I was never sure what he could hear or see, it was important the house felt and sounded as normal as possible. His deterioration was now very rapid and it was hard to tell to what degree he was suffering and what he was aware of. I switched the television to the sports channel just in case he wanted to watch it, and I chatted all day to him, telling him the local tales I'd heard, and reading the papers out loud.

John had always been very particular about his personal hygiene and I wanted to make sure that he retained that dignity. I bathed and shaved him every morning, changed his pyjamas and plumped up his pillows.

'There you are,' I'd say cheerfully. 'You do look handsome.'

Sometimes he looked at me and I recognized something in his eyes; at other times he tried to reach for my hand, but more often than not there was no response at all in those last weeks.

It was hard for the girls to witness because they loved John and wanted to be involved in his care. Erin was living at home and nursed him beautifully when I had to go out. For someone so young, still only sixteen, she was a tower of strength during those difficult days. Somehow, between us all, John knew he had love surrounding him.

Watching him deteriorating to such a degree was heartbreaking. For all the struggles I'd faced during my life – the cruelty, the beatings, the homelessness and poverty – nothing had prepared me for this. It was my biggest ever challenge.

The Macmillan nurse came once a week and she always stopped for coffee and a chat. It was a big help to have her around. She was very experienced and we became firm friends.

'Thanks,' I always said at the end. 'What you're doing makes a big difference.'

One day she gave me a hug and said, 'I love coming here. You always make *me* feel better, Judy.'

I was bowled over by that.

It was important to me that John was included in everything. Sometimes we had visitors who talked over his head, as if he wasn't there. When they left I asked them please to come in the next time remembering that John needed to feel part of what was going on. This woke them up and they apologized. The visits became better.

When we were alone I lay down on the bed beside John and put my arms around him. He had always liked me to stroke his head. I told him how happy he had made me and how lucky we were to have found each other. Although we had only been together a short while we had a bond that very few people ever find. I hoped that he could hear me, but if he couldn't I was sure he would know somehow.

It was very hard at the end when John stopped eating. I tried everything, even baby food, but he just couldn't swallow any more. The district nurse came regularly to help me get him out of bed to prevent bed sores and to bathe him. He was now doubly incontinent and needed many changes during the day. Seeing him as ill as this tore me up and I began to hope that he wasn't lucid. I knew he'd be devastated if he realized what was going on.

In the evenings, once I had settled him down for the night, I needed some peace and tranquillity. I often went for walks in the woods and sat by our favourite old tree. While resting my head on its trunk I was unable to stop my tears falling. I looked up at the stars and asked them please to look after John, to help him not to suffer any more and take him safely to the place he wanted to be. The rustling of the leaves and the twinkling of the stars reassured me, and as I walked back indoors I felt my courage renewed, and knew that our love would never die.

# Chapter Thirty-three

*I*t was now the end of September 1991 and John had been bed-ridden for three months. I was having trouble getting even the tiniest drop of fluid into him. I could only moisten his lips with water. He had developed pneumonia and was finding it difficult to breathe. The district nurse came as usual and lifted him out of bed so that I could change the sheets. John was so tiny, he was like a bag of bones and his face was no bigger than my hand. One day the nurse must have hurt him a little for he cried the word 'Mummy'. He looked at me and I knew he was aware his time was almost up.

On the morning of 2 October John's breathing changed and I realized that he had taken a turn for the worse. I washed and shaved him and plumped up his pillows. I sensed that today was the day he would be free, and I wanted to share every last moment with him. I chatted and stroked his head and played his favourite piece of classical music, Beethoven's *Pastoral Symphony*. Then I lay next to him and wrapped my arms around his decimated body. His head rested on my shoulder and we stayed like that for a couple of hours. Slowly his breathing became shallower and at three o'clock in the afternoon, as I held him close, I kissed him goodbye as he slipped away.

Afterwards I sat there in disbelief. It didn't feel real. I felt as though my soul had gone with him. I had a sense of suspended animation. After a while – I'm not sure how long – I went to see Erin. She had been working very late at the restaurant the night before and was sleeping. I knocked on her door and when she saw me she just knew. We walked down to the lounge together and held hands.

'He has a smile on his face, Mum, he's gone where he is no longer in pain.'

I called Dr Bennett and the health visitor and they both came over immediately. It is the law that when someone dies at home the doctor has to investigate and write a report. They took care of those practicalities and both offered me their help any time.

For the next few days I kept myself busy with everything that needed to be organized. One day, earlier on in his illness, John had asked me if I would take his funeral service when the time came and I'd promised faithfully that I would. He had also told me about a school friend of his who was now an undertaker and he'd asked for this friend, Brian, to arrange his funeral. I contacted him and he came from Fife to arrange everything. John wanted to be cremated but the nearest crematorium was one hundred and twenty miles away in Perth. Brian drove John's body down there in preparation for the service a few days later.

I wanted the funeral to be a celebration of John's life, as I'm sure he would have wanted. I asked everyone to wear brightly coloured clothes as a sign that it was to be an uplifting service. John's colleagues came, along with his elderly aunts, his sons, friends, and Carrie and Erin. The congregation for the service looked as though a rainbow had hit it. At the close of my dedication I reminded everyone of John's love for the sun.

'Wherever you see the sun you'll know that John will be there.'

And as if on cue, streams of sunlight filtered through the windows of the church.

As John's coffin was taken into the crematorium and before the curtains closed I blew him a kiss. We had been married for just a month short of four years.

# Chapter Thirty-four

*A*fter the stress of caring for John for all those months, I desperately needed some time to myself, to gather my thoughts. I packed a few things in a case and put a childhood toy of John's – a koala bear called Blinkie Bill – in my pocket. It was comforting to have such a personal possession of his with me, almost as though I was taking him along. I drove down south to Chester, stopping at B & Bs along the way, and, still in shock, stayed a day and then drove home again. It was only the very beginning, but that week away was the start of the healing process.

Back at the house there were things that needed to be done to get back to normal. It was a very strange feeling moving back into our bedroom. Sleeping in our bed without John was going to take a long time to get used to. Sometimes, just doing something normal like making a cup of tea would set me off crying. John had made sure that the house was in my name so that I would be secure after he had gone. As I looked out of the window and saw the garden he had so lovingly tended I often felt his presence. When I took the dog for a walk up to the hills I sat and talked to John, feeling especially close to him there. I was blessed that I had found my soul mate and although our time together was short we had treasured every moment. Most of all, I was glad that we had gone to Africa together and he'd realized his childhood dream.

After a week I went to collect John's ashes. It was a highly emotional moment and I found it hard to accept that my loving husband was in that very small vase. I brought the ashes home and discussed with the girls what to do with them. I wanted John to be part of the countryside he loved so much so I bought some spring bulbs, and in our very special place by the riverside, exactly where John and I used to sit, I planted a garden. It was a wonderful thought that it would be there for years to come – beautiful flowers in the place that John loved – as though he was there as well.

I was still numb with shock and grief for several months. I floated around in a daze, going through the motions of normal life but feeling separate from it at the same time. I decided it would be good for me to get back to teaching and prepare for our end of year show. The students were raring to go and I revamped the old pantomime 'Cinderella and Friends' that we had put on in Sheerwater. The new show was called 'Cinderella's Dream', with Erin playing the part of Cinders. I decided that the money raised from the show would establish a 'John Westwater Nursing Fund'.

While I was caring for John there was a lot of equipment that would have made it easier. A monitor system, similar to the baby monitors all mothers use, would have been handy. Special drinking cups, air-pressurized beds, wheelchairs – there was all sorts of stuff that was not available for the home care of terminally ill people but that would have made life easier. I asked Dr Bennett if he would administer the money we raised and buy all the necessary equipment. There is very little a carer can do in the later stages, but simply making your loved one as comfortable as possible makes all the difference.

Because John died in service the Health and Safety Executive gave a benefit of two years' salary. Before he died, John had nominated me to receive this and a few weeks after the funeral a cheque arrived. I couldn't believe it. The cheque was for £44,000. It was more money than I had ever even thought about having but it meant nothing. Money was such an impossible exchange for not having John with me any more that I didn't know what to do with it. In the end I left the envelope on my coffee table and forgot all about it.

One night I arrived home absolutely exhausted from taking a rehearsal. I settled down in front of the open fire. Erin was out and so it was just the dog and me. I reached for my coffee and suddenly there was the cheque. It had been lying on the coffee table for weeks.

I began to think about what I could possibly do with it. Then, I switched on the television. There was a programme about the troubles in South Africa. Nelson Mandela had been released from prison in February 1990 and was negotiating with President F. W. de Klerk to bring the apartheid system to an end and to hold free elections in which black people would be allowed to vote for the first time, but it was not a straightforward path. I knew from living there that despite all the changes taking place, the children of the townships would be the last ones to be considered. They still received only token education and had very few resources. Years of living under the suppression of apartheid, grinding poverty and township violence had rendered them valueless.

I felt so passionate that I found myself saying 'To be able to spread their wings and fly in a new country they need care and attention.' Then I realized I was speaking out loud to the television. I sat for a minute or two looking at the screen. Something had hit home. Answers often arrive in mysterious ways and this is how I found mine. I picked up the cheque and as I stood up with it in my hand all the fog seemed to clear away.

When I was homeless there was a day I was thrown off a whites-only bus. I was a skinny kid with a dark suntan and matted hair after months of living on the streets so the conductor was convinced that I was a coloured girl. No matter how much I protested he had thrown me off the bus. I sat in the dirt outside Joubert Park, nursing my bruises, and fumed to myself about the unfairness of it all. I wrote in the dirt with my finger: 'One day I will come back and change things for kids like me.' One day.

That promise echoed down the years and I stared at the cheque as my mind cleared. 'This is the opportunity and John has given it to me,' I said to myself. 'It's a perfect tribute.'

I'd had to overcome many challenges in my life and losing John was the hardest of them all. I learned from a very young age that you have to live life as it is before you can make it how you'd like it to be. I was now by myself again. My children were grown up with lives of their own. It was the perfect time for me to make a new life for myself too. And here, suddenly, I had the means to make good the promise I made in Johannesburg all those years ago. Everything I had done so far, all my schools and teaching, had been the building blocks of that pledge, slowly, slowly growing until the time was ripe.

Years of running successful schools had proved to me that children in need could benefit from what I had to offer. My unique method worked. I had lived an isolated street life and been an unseen child living in a township. I had the 'living that life' qualifications as well as the piece of paper from LAMDA.

During our evening chats under our favourite tree John and I had idly discussed what we would do if we ever found ourselves with lots of money. I said I would create projects throughout the world to help as many vulnerable children as I could and John had agreed – especially after all he'd seen in Kenya. Standing there alone with the cheque in my hand it felt as though John was by my side giving me a thumbs up.

I couldn't wait for Erin to come home so that I could share the news with her. She couldn't believe how excited I was as I told her all about how I was going to turn John's money into something worthwhile for vulnerable kids in South Africa.

'Let's you and me go together,' I suggested. 'You can help me to set something up.'

Erin had helped so much with caring for John during his illness that I felt it was just the break she needed. She was delighted to be involved and we managed to persuade her boss at the restaurant to give her time off work.

Once I've got an idea in my head, I don't hang about. I decided we were going in a fortnight. I phoned Jude, David and Carrie and they were all chuffed to bits with the idea. So, without more ado, Erin and I packed and set off for Africa. It was November 1991. As our plane lifted off the runway I knew I was stepping into a new life again. There would be many more challenges to overcome but I was well equipped and looking forward to facing them head on.

'Where are we going to stay when we get there?' Erin asked suddenly.

'A little place called Hillbrow,' I replied.

The place where it all began. The place where I'd lived on the streets. The place where I'd be able to help all those street kids just like me.

# *Epilogue*

*February 1993*

*I*t was 8:30 in the morning and I had just packed our Volkswagen Combi with all the materials I needed that day for the classes at my new project in Khayelitsha. I knew the students were very excited. They hadn't wanted me to leave at all the week before, and I had promised them faithfully that I would be back that day at any cost.

Khayelitsha, which means 'new home', was a dirty, overcrowded, lawless township roughly twenty miles from the centre of Cape Town. Its five-mile span housed over half a million people, with thousands more flocking there each month, looking for work in the city. The sprawling township was built on a rubbish dump, with thousands of shacks made from tin, bits of wood, cardboard and corrugated iron, flanked by dusty red roads. There was no electricity and very little water. All day, and often for most of the night, lines of mothers with babies on their backs and water carriers on their heads, snaked the huge distances to the nearest communal tap. In the summer the tiny shacks became ovens, baking under the relentless sun, while in the rainy season they were flooded or washed away.

The pungent smell of smoke and cooking meat filled the endless maze of alleyways, and naked children and skinny dogs hung around the open fires. Many of the shacks were turned into makeshift shops where people tried to sell whatever they could find in the city. In the many shabeens (drinking houses), men gathered and drank to fill their days in place of the work they couldn't find. Stabbings and shootings were a regular occurrence.

In the run up to the 1994 elections for a new South Africa, unemployment had reached 80 percent and township violence was running out of control. Domestic brutality, rape, child abuse and murders increased, but police presence was minimal and in this climate, vigilante activities grew. Anarchy raged.

Once on the road I turned on the radio and was shocked at the news. 'Our nation's taxi wars have flared up again in earnest,' the announcer said. 'We are reaching a climate of terror. More than seventy buses have been targeted by operators of illegal taxis, outraged that bus companies are allowed to undercut fares. Several passengers have been killed.'

Alarmingly, the announcer went on to say that trouble was expected for anyone trying to get into Khayelitsha that day.

The roots of the taxi wars were embedded in the apartheid system, which provided no adequate transport for migrants to travel into the city. To get to work many of them created their own taxi services. This escalated and new independent associations developed. The result was war, with the different associations fighting to control the most lucrative routes, and it was not uncommon for 'hit squad' taxi drivers to carry shotguns and shoot rival drivers. Many of the illegal drivers were poor and competition was furious. Even the legitimate ones caused further riots by poaching fares.

I realized it was going to be serious that morning, but I'd made a promise and had no intention of breaking it.

As I drove onto the bridge leading into Khayelitsha it was mayhem and I had to stop. There were people everywhere, some running in wild confusion. Others were diving for cover as shots rang out. I needed to get through this chaos to take the turn-off to Site C, where my project was, but the whole road was blocked. I didn't dare drive on because clouds of dust from the dirt roads made it impossible to see. Warring taxis skidded and parried as the occupants violently attacked each other. My stomach began to churn. Sitting with the engine running I felt really vulnerable. I heard the sound of chanting behind me then suddenly noticed a group of ten angry men moving towards my van. It dawned on me far too late that because I was driving a white Combi they probably believed that I too was a rogue taxi. I was in big trouble.

Then, from out of nowhere, a broad, stocky man dressed in tribal gear with his face covered in war paint darted in front of my windscreen shouting obscenities in his native Xhosa language. His face was running with sweat and contorted with anger, his body stiff and ridged with clenched muscles. He waved his fist at me and then lifted his arm. He was holding a tribal assegai (a long-handled spear) in his hand, its blade glinting bright in the sun. He moved closer to the van, raised his arm ready to smash through the window and pressed his face right on to the windscreen, squashing his features in a truly menacing gesture. He seemed to be the leader of the gang as this action prompted the encroaching intimidators to surround the van.

I was desperate and just about to ram the gears into reverse, hoping that the gang would jump out of the way, when out of the blue, the man suddenly widened his eyes and smiled at me. This threw me completely. I didn't understand. What on earth was he smiling for? He took a step back and began to dance in tribal fashion. It was really bizarre and an alarming thought flashed though my mind: was this the dance of death? Then to my disbelief he waved his free hand and, with the assegai above his head, he shouted 'Mama Jooody, Mama Jooody. Hello Mama Jooody,' and ushered me to one side away from the riots.

People in the crowd were peering to see what was going on and nudging each other and pointing. All the time the man walked beside the van pointing his assegai horizontally at the crowd of raging taxi drivers so that they had to let me to pass. My mouth was as dry as the dust and my heart raced. But it was working. Slowly, the crowds parted and lined up on both sides of the road. I couldn't believe they were letting me through. I had never seen the man before, I was sure of it, but I wasn't stopping to ask any questions.

It was like having a red carpet laid down for me. As I turned the corner into Site C I began to breathe normally at last. I knew I was lucky to be alive. I'd been working in the Cape Town townships for about two years and somehow this man must have heard about me.

'Mama Jooody,' he said at last, with a little farewell bow.

As I got out of the van a huge crowd surrounded me. There were kids, old men, women with babies on their backs. I recognized the children from the project but it seemed that the whole village had also come that morning to welcome me. They were so concerned about my safety that they picked me up, carrying me in a mass of soft hands and shoulders towards the project. I looked over and saw my protector disappear into the distance.

There was a long history of false promises and failed good intentions in Khayelitsha, and over time the community's faith and trust had been shattered. To begin with they were amazed that I came when I said I would. But as far as I was concerned, my word was my bond. Now they all knew I kept my promises. Their fight had become my fight too. I would do anything to help.

By this time I had opened centres in the townships of Soweto, Alexandra and Sebokeng, as well as Khayelitsha, and also a separate project at the Market Theatre Laboratory, an organized community theatre group that nurtures young talent. John's money had been a great start and now I was raising more.

As the people of Khayelitsha carried me along that day, they all burst into song, a typical African stress reliever. I knew that they were singing something about me because I could pick out my name amongst the Xhosa words. It was an incredible feeling. Here I was, in a vast sea of violence and deprivation being so loved and cherished. Every person I helped cancelled out some of the pain from my own past. All the misery I had endured finally made sense. It would let me help these people. Their welcome touched me deeply. They had nothing. They lived in constant fear with no way out of their darkness, yet they saw me, a white woman as a light in their lives. This poor, black community was behind me one hundred percent and I was never going to let them down.

A young girl came up to me, held my hand and said 'Mama Judy, you are our mother.'

'Let's get to work, then,' I said. 'We have such a lot to do.'

# PEGASUS CHILDREN'S TRUST

Judy has opened seven centres for street children to date and works tirelessly to keep them flourishing. When she is not in South Africa helping her co-workers, she is fund raising in Great Britain.

For more information about Judy, Pegasus Children's Trust, her work in South Africa and how you can help, please visit www.streetkid.co.uk or write to:

Pegasus Children's Trust
PO Box 5711
118A Bruce Gardens
Inverness
IV1 9AN
Scotland

Email: kidsinflight@tiscali.co.uk
Charity registration number: SC 037365

# Acknowledgements

I would like to express my deep gratitude and sincere appreciation to all who have shared my journey in the making of this book. First and foremost a huge thank you and big hugs for the star, my editorial director Susanna Abbott, for her quiet strength, true friendship, dedicated commitment and gentle guidance. Sincere thanks also to all at Harper Element for having faith in my story. Much appreciation goes to Sara Sheriden for all her hard work. A big 'thank you' to A1 plus publicist Laura Summers; her professionalism, tenacity and warm friendship is truly appreciated. A very special word of thanks goes to Gill Paul for her most valuable input, her sensitivity and caring respect.

I wish to offer my sincere thanks to Nour Arthur and all at the Charity and Sponsorship department of Virgin Atlantic Airways, the team at London Heathrow's Thistle Hotel and the gang at Thomas Cook, Inverness for their utmost support of my work and fantastic care. And finally, huge hugs and sincere thanks for Peta Nightingale, my lovely agent and treasured friend. Her professional eye, sensitive ear and deep understanding have led the way. Thank you everyone.